BOOK OF JOBS

C.B. MURPHY

ZOOGRAPHICO PRESS

Copyright © 2022, C.B. Murphy

All rights reserved. No part of this publication may be reproduced, distributed, or transmitted in any form or by any means, including photocopying, recording, digital scanning, or other electronic or mechanical methods, without the prior written permission of the publisher, except in the case of brief quotations embodied in critical reviews and certain other noncommercial uses permitted by copyright law. For permission requests, please address Zoographico Press.

Published 2022
Zoographico Press
Marine on St. Croix, MN
zoographicopress@gmail.com

Print ISBN: 978-0-934150-04-0

Library of Congress Control Number: 2022914908

Book Design by Kelly Harminc

Printed in the United States of America

BOOK OF JOBS

CONTENTS

1 INTRODUCTION

CHAPTER 1
4 PRIEST

CHAPTER 2
8 PAPERBOY

CHAPTER 3
12 BAKERY

CHAPTER 4
18 OCCULTIST

CHAPTER 5
24 CADDY

CHAPTER 6
28 MONA FILMS

CHAPTER 7
34 DAIRY FACTORY

CHAPTER 8
38 UNDERGROUND FILMMAKER

CHAPTER 9
44 NUDE MODEL

CHAPTER 10
48 DISHWASHER

CHAPTER 11
52 HOSPITAL JANITOR

CHAPTER 12
56 UNDERGROUND FILMMAKER II

CHAPTER 13
60 COMMERCIAL FILM

CHAPTER 14
66 IPMC ORDER CLERK

CHAPTER 15
72 PRECIOUS METALS TRADER

INTRODUCTION

I dream about work nearly every night. Some dreams are funny, others are nightmares. In my dreams there is always something I haven't done, someone I haven't called back, something I failed to deliver, or someone coming after me with a complex work-related grudge. People don't pat me on the back in my dreams. I almost never wake up with the feeling of satisfaction of having done a "good job."

One night I dreamed about getting a new job as an assistant to some hotshot in LA. I think it was in advertising—a field I once thought suited me. It probably didn't help that I had watched the season finale of *Mad Men* before I went to bed. Don had a toothache and his pouty French-Canadian wife wanted to be an actress, not a housewife. Oh, and his firm had outgrown its office.

POOR DON DRAPER.

In my dream I had to find my house, but I needed clothes. I sneaked into the Coast Guard's exclusive, clothing-optional, executive swim club locker room to steal some. However, I neglected to swipe shoes. When I met up with my new boss (a suave version of a fast-talking Jack Black), I had to listen to his female companion (a cross between Roseanne and Phyllis Diller) gush about the latest Sbarro's ad campaign where people spout obscenities. Something about eating babies gets bleeped out, but you can still read their lips.

"Hysterical!" she says. Then they comment on my outfit and, since we are all so urbane, I admit I pilfered it. They are not shocked, but point out I am not wearing shoes.

"Why didn't you steal shoes?" the hip, funny woman asks and then **chases me around the room with a meat cleaver.**

I have had many jobs—over twenty, depending on which I'm willing to count. But why illustrate them in cartoons? Let's put it another way: why would someone illustrate their life with cartoons if they're not a comedian?

PERHAPS THIS IS A QUESTION FOR THERAPY.

CHAPTER 1
PRIEST

Big Irish-Catholic families circa the mid-1950s had a few built-in agendas. Like many nostalgic ethnicities, the American Irish tended to have large families, even after children were no longer needed to work the fields. Huge was good and a point of pride, especially for the patriarchs who didn't have to get pregnant. My parents did their part by having seven boys and three girls.

In the Irish-Catholic template, the patriarch could assign various offspring to their future jobs. This was how my dad became a dentist (his other choice was real estate), and how he expected he would one day run his own family. Offering up children to religious vocations, such as the priesthood or nunnery, was integral to community status, especially if you had an ample brood. This tradition served several purposes. It greased the wheels of the Catholic machine by providing low-cost local labor, and it served as a kind of down payment against the cumulative family sins that might keep some members out of heaven. Not terribly unlike buying indulgences that so pissed off Martin Luther.

Sexism being fully integrated, the highest rank was always a priest, with a monastic brother coming in second. A nun was third choice. This was the way it was in my dad's family. His older brother, Claire, became a priest. My mom's Irish-Catholic clan had more girls than boys, so they contributed Gloria to the Sisters of Charity and she became Sister Helen Michael. (The nuns had to take a new name, but the priests and brothers didn't.)

The sales pitch to the chosen child was embodied in the word "vocation." A vocation was a mysterious "call from God," an honor bestowed upon a family. The tricky part was that the parents had to nudge the chosen child in the direction of thinking they were meant for such an occupation. You wouldn't want a troublemaker to feel inspired.

Perhaps in the old country, the unwritten rule was the first male child had to run the farm, so he wasn't the best choice for a religious calling. **As the second male child, I was chosen to be the priest.**

I was smart enough and, at an early age, compliant enough, so the assumption was that I could handle the role, which was part theatrical performer and part community organizer. If people were telling the truth about human life being a flash in the pan before eternity, then becoming a priest was an excellent way to ensure a front row seat to viewing the face of God—supposedly the full-time occupation of those who made it to heaven. Not that it was easy to imagine sitting on a cloud and looking at a serene giant face as all that fulfilling (or fun), but that's where the word "mystery" came in.

THAT WORD HAD A LOT OF WORK TO DO.

I did see that in becoming a priest, everything would be provided by Mother Church for my entire life. I would float above many of the worries that complicated my parents' lives, especially money and relatives. As a pre-pubescent boy, I viewed the commitment to a lifetime of celibacy as a win-win. I could skip dating, marrying, buying a house, having kids, and then worrying about how to pay for their college educations. It looked like a pretty good deal.

To encourage my mystical "vocation," I set up an altar in our basement, complete with a tabernacle, chalices, and vestments. I even improvised Holy Communion wafers by meticulously squishing Wonder Bread into thin white discs. It sounds vaguely blasphemous, pretending to be a servant of God, but my family took it as proof that I was indeed called to it.

It's hard to remember how I segued from priest to anything-but-priest, though when puberty hit, the whole setup stopped sounding so great. I would miss girls, dating, fast cars, drinking, girls, making out, and generally the fun of being "bad." The other issue at play was that the 1950s model of the big Irish-Catholic family was rapidly being corroded (literally by acid) as the skeptical 1960s kicked in.

REBELLION WAS AFOOT.

CHAPTER 2
PAPERBOY

My first real job was being employed by my older brother as an adjunct-associate paperboy. Jerry had a route delivering the morning *Detroit Free Press* before it merged with the afternoon *Detroit News* in 1987. The idea, probably my dad's, was the family institution of The Route would be passed down from Murphy boy to Murphy boy. **My sisters were on a separate trajectory.**

Our territory comprised two parts of Bloomfield Hills, Michigan—the "Catholic ghetto" of Greenwich Green and the Jewish neighborhood of Westchester. Like thousands of other subdivisions in the United States, both areas stole their names from English boroughs and towns, trying desperately to sound pleasant and bucolic. The only thing that separated Westchester from the Catholic education compound (which included a parish house, elementary school, a boy's high school, a girl's high school, residences for the Sisters of the Immaculate Heart of Mary, and another for the Christian Brothers of Ireland) was a series of citizen-constructed barricades. There were four streets blocked off this way, crude amateurish structures easily visible from the north-facing windows of St. Regis Elementary School. The low fences were made from tree stumps connected by wooden planks, then everything was painted white, as if apologizing for the outrageousness. There was an opening to allow pedestrians through, but basically it looked like something you would see in Northern Ireland during the Troubles.

While my older brother was in charge, I don't remember ever being paid in real money, though it's hard to believe I wasn't. What I do remember is how he would treat me and my brothers to comics and candy at the local store. Wampum for the savages, to use a sad analogy. By the time he passed The Route on to me, I realized that even though we had worked side by side for years, I never understood the finer points of how the business operated. I was good at the delivery part, which included getting my two younger brothers up at 5:30 AM and out the door in all weather.

WHAT TRIPPED ME UP WAS THE DREADED "COLLECTING" PART OF THE JOB.

Collecting described the task of walking up to peoples' houses and asking for money. These were folks who gladly read your paper every morning, but on Friday afternoon treated you like a Jehovah's Witness, or worse. It meant a young man (me) would have to go up to a house that ostensibly subscribed to the paper and get them to actually pay (in cash!) for the weekly or monthly delivery. The words collect, collecting, or collection still trigger anxiety today. I suspect my fear of economic transactions began here. This was supposed to be a simpler, more honest time, but many of my customers had no compunctions about taking advantage of a dumb kid. I quickly learned that a punched hole in a payment card didn't mean anything to someone who didn't want to pay.

One excuse was the simple, "Can you come back later?" Then there was, "I didn't get my paper on Wednesday (or Friday or . . .)." How could I argue against that, especially if it was on one of my brothers' sections of The Route? Even if it was on mine, I would have had a hard time saying, "No, you're wrong. I know I delivered on those days." It was not uncommon for them to claim they had "stopped the paper weeks ago." But had they really? And if they had, whose mistake was it? There was no proof they had made that call. Their accusatory tone implied they had suffered in receiving unwanted papers. It was as if I owed them for the inconvenience.

One of the highlights of The Route was the day I found The Dead Guy. I came upon a car stopped in the middle of the street with the door open and a man in a suit slumped over. I was certain I was the first to discover a mob hit. Me—the paperboy. This would surely make the local news. But when I saw a cop car with flashing lights approach, I slunk away and watched from a vantage point while they forced the guy to stand up and lean on the car.

HE WASN'T DEAD AFTER ALL. HE WAS DEAD DRUNK.

CHAPTER 3
BAKERY

My first job where I got an actual printed paycheck was at Miami Bakery, located in a strip mall in Southfield, Michigan. It was named Miami Bakery for reasons still somewhat unclear, though I think it had to do with Miami being associated with Jews. Although I never heard anyone say, "This is a Jewish bakery," their goods had names I had never heard of: *hamantaschen*, *kichel*, *pletzlach*, and *challah*. They also made a full line of generic cookies and birthday cakes for special order.

The bakery was co-owned by a Catholic, Mr. Nichols, and a Jewish man, Mr. Winkler. Mr. Winkler seemed to be semi-retired, as he only worked Sunday mornings when the Catholics went to church. Over time, a number of my friends and family ended up working there too. It started with my friend Greg, followed by my younger brothers, Dan and Peter. Greg got his brother Mark hired as well. It's not like it was a big place—we just dominated the lowest rung of after-school and Saturday wash-up boys.

After we punched in, we changed into white shirts, pants, and aprons they provided, in a tiny room that was actually the bathroom. Our main job was scraping and washing the tall aluminum racks that held baking pans. By the end of the shift, you had thoroughly soaked your white uniform. We also scraped the pans that went into the ovens and then placed them on a wheeled cart that went to Albert, a thin and elegant African-American man, who washed them in a huge sink with his long, graceful fingers. We sometimes relieved Albert for his breaks.

In the summer we could wash the racks outside; otherwise, we rinsed them inside by the back freezers and storage room. On Fridays, we had to peel onions and crush them into small pieces with a handheld chopper. These would go into the onion rolls, another Jewish specialty I had never heard of.

I LEARNED ALL KINDS OF THINGS AT THE BAKERY—AND NOT ALL OF THEM WERE RELATED TO BAKED GOODS.

The storage room opened to the alley, and it was here that we got to know a series of deliverymen, including a dapper African-

American man with huge muscles named Claude. Claude introduced us to the word "nookie" as in "Did you get any nookie recently?" By the time we deciphered what nookie was, we knew it wasn't cool to say you hadn't gotten any ever.

Another older worker, a greasy white guy named Neil, showed me the first pornography I ever saw. Out in the alley, he opened up the trunk of his car to reveal a cache of magazines full of women spread-eagled, with no attempt at art.

Mr. Nichols had a son named Charlie, who was approximately my age. He was a pale, lean, red-haired kid with a perpetually angry expression on his horsey face. As an owner's son, he fought to differentiate himself from the hired rabble, though we mostly did the same work. He wasn't our boss, but he liked to think he was. I wasn't sure if Charlie hated everyone or took a particular dislike to our little gang, but he became our villain, the scourge of our existence. Greg seemed to love taunting him and nicknamed him the "Red Devil" because of his mop of unruly ginger hair and dark temperament.

I speculated our conflict with the Red Devil had something to do with class. Our gang came from Catholic families, like his, but we went to an upscale, all-boys private school. Charlie went to a tougher public school in a blue-collar area. Our prep academy put a major focus on everyone going to college; Charlie's fate seemed predetermined: he'd take over his dad's half of the bakery. He might be here forever, while we were blithely using the job for pocket money. Forget about saving for college. We worked because that's what you did.

Most of the kids in my school were "frats" who wore button-down Oxford shirts and penny loafers (or some variation of wingtip shoes). Greasers, on the other hand, tended to wear their hair long but slicked back with Brylcream into a "ducktail." Sometimes they fluffed it up on top like John Travolta in *Grease*. Their pants were tighter than frat khakis, and their thin black shoes ended in sharp points that were reputedly useful in brawls (which we had only seen in the stylized dancing of *West Side Story*). Charlie qualified as a greaser. None of us had ever seen him fight, but he carried himself like a streetfighter, with legs wide apart to accommodate his massive *cajones*.

On Sunday mornings, we had to be at work by 5 AM. These mornings belonged to Mr. Winkler. Picture a guy with wavy, thinning, slicked-back hair and a pencil-thin mustache like a big-band conductor. He was going for the Frank Sinatra style—classiness with a touch of sleaze, always working to make an impression on the ladies.

Midmorning, Mr. Winkler stopped all work and made the entire staff a breakfast of eggs, sausage, bagels, and coffee. We all gathered around the huge butcher block table and he told us stories about his past. Inevitably, he tried to get us to talk about the adventurous sex lives he thought us "young bucks" had. He imagined we were out every Saturday night with our girlfriends getting "nookie," and he expected to hear about it, as if we owed him stories in payment for breakfast.

We were not opposed to being seen this way, but the truth was, the wildest we got was drinking beer on the golf course or "pool hopping" (jumping into strangers' swimming pools while they were sleeping); our social lives were not yet integrated with the world of girls.

BUT THE TRUTH WAS NOT WHAT MR. WINKLER WANTED TO HEAR.

So, while I personally found this embarrassing, I learned from Greg how to toss out coy references to back-seat intercourse at the drive-in and other make-out spots, stuff we picked up from watching 1950s creature features—and Winkler ate it up. He would wiggle his eyebrows and ask for more details about our imaginary dates. And since the Red Devil never worked on Sundays, a good time was had by all.

IT WAS ALMOST WORTH GETTING UP AT 5 AM.

CHAPTER 4
OCCULTIST

While this section isn't exactly about a job, my experience in the Free Thinkers Association (the FTA) led me to question everything around me, which affected many of the choices I made later.

First, let me explain how my all-boys Catholic high school worked. At Brother Rice High School in Bloomfield Hills, Michigan, the Christian Brothers of Ireland categorized each boy by a number from one to seven. **I assume it was based on some kind of test, but I don't remember taking one.**

The homerooms were numbered: the smartest kids—the eggheads, nerds, and socially awkward brainiacs—were in 107, and the lowest achievers were in 101. The latter nicknamed itself The Zoo, making their low status a point of macho pride.

My friend, Greg, was in 105, where the socially savvy had decided "normal" people were, which made being "too smart" as much a social stigma as being "too dumb." According to 105 logic, there was even something wrong with 106. This group, mostly comprised of preppy elitists who wore penny loafers, were snobs. Having a friendship with someone in 105 that predated high school was my doorway to "normal" teenage life, the kind one hoped to have in a mid-1960s all-boys Catholic school in our upscale suburb of Detroit.

The Free Thinkers Association was the brainchild of one of my egghead friends in 107, a guy named Ed Sears. He was a strange, quiet kid whose head looked like a model for the elongated craniums on a Mayan wall fresco. Bob Mulcrone, another founding member, was a nervous guy with chronic sinus problems and an odd, pear-shaped body. Ed structured our meetings not unlike the Victorian study group that gathered to witness Rod Taylor's experiments in *The Time Machine* (1960).

IN THE LATE 1960S, IT WASN'T EASY TO GET INFORMATION ABOUT WHAT WAS HAPPENING IN THE REAL WORLD.

We only had mainstream outlets—television news, the radio, *Time* Magazine, the *Detroit Free Press*, and the public library. Nevertheless, we heard strange rumblings. Things were happening "out there." Rebellion was afoot. We had some notion that the beatniks caricatured by the Maynard G. Kreps character on *The Many Loves of Dobie Gillis* TV show were morphing into members of something called the "hippie movement."

It was somewhat socially awkward to study occult topics in each others' basements, especially since we didn't drive yet and had to be chauffeured to and from our respective houses. The feeling was probably similar to what the Dungeons & Dragons crowd had to suffer through, with parents worried about black magic and drugs. An adult would often yell downstairs, "Are you guys okay down there?" These worries weren't totally unfounded, given our purpose was to study all things taboo and mysterious.

At first it was an exclusively 107 thing, but Greg from 105 became fascinated by my stories and wanted in so we made a deal. **I would get him into the mystery cult, and he would get me into his "normal" high school social circle.** This included a friend with a license and a hot GTO convertible we could drive up and down the infamous Woodward Strip.

An avid reader, Ed introduced us to the world of Eastern religions—Hinduism, Buddhism, and their various esoteric offspring, like Theosophy and Vedanta. Since Catholics frowned on taking any of these religions "seriously" as valid paths to meaning, it was thrilling to flit from them to UFOs, Madame Blavatsky, and Aleister Crowley. Basically, anything that wasn't Catholic interested us.

We studied the budding hippie movement and Ed found a cult called Kerista, which had a commune on a Caribbean island where members practiced "free love." It seemed an option, if all else failed. We also heard people were "taking drugs," but none of us knew what kind or what for. Ed found some information on sodium pentothal ("truth serum") and plotted to get some to use in quest of truth.

Discouraged by the unsuccessful sodium pentothal acquisition, Ed discovered hypnotism. Thanks to Madame Blavatsky (*The Secret Doctrine*, 1888), our brains were filled with ideas of alternate realities, other planes of being, and the rich and chaotic world of reincarnation. Ed got the idea that hypnotism could be used as a tool for mental retrogression and could take one of us back to the "place before we were born."

SURPRISINGLY, HYPNOTISM ISN'T ALL THAT DIFFICULT.

I bought a cheap hypno-disk from the gag section in the back of a comic book. After a few trial runs, it was clear Greg was the best subject and I was the best hypnotist. We were ready to discover a new world.

One day I started the usual way by using the spinning disk. "You're getting sleepy," etcetera. When Greg's face fell slack, and I was sure he was under, I said, "You're getting younger and younger. Younger. Younger."

I tried my best to be patient, since I wasn't sure what kind of effort it took for a person to travel back before they were born. Greg's eyes opened wide as he stared at something none of us could see. Then he leaned forward and squinted. "What do you see?" I asked.

"I'm trying...to read...the words." He spoke slowly as if under stress. We were as excited as Columbus thinking he had discovered a new route to India. "Describe where you are."

"It's a room," he said slowly, as if speaking was difficult. "And there's an altar with a hand on it, a large statue of a hand. There's some writing underneath it."

I handed Greg a pad and a pencil, and he began transcribing without looking at what he wrote. We expected him to write out something fantastic, perhaps something in an ancient hieroglyphic language, even extraterrestrial in nature. I was ready to be world famous when I took the pad of paper from his hands. But all that was there were scribbles.

THOUGH DISAPPOINTED, WE WERE AWED AT HOW CLOSE WE GOT TO CRACKING THE MYSTERY OF HUMAN EXISTENCE.

CHAPTER 5
CADDY

During that time, there was a popular concept that caddying had more than one benefit for a young man. On one level, it was a physical challenge that would "make a man out of you." Although there was some truth to this, being a mute pack animal for men you assumed were wealthier than your father was an odd initiation into manhood. I'm not sure why I assumed these men were richer than my dad, who was a dentist with ten children in private schools, living in the same neighborhood as these guys. I guess it was because my dad hadn't carved out time for this kind of leisure activity, which led to the unspoken assumption that we couldn't afford it.

The basic idea of caddying was that you were supposed to see how the wealthy lived and, despite being treated as a servant, this would somehow motivate you to want to be like them. Following in the footsteps of my older brother, I left Miami Bakery and became an Oakland Hills Country Club caddy.

At the time, golf seemed to be about celebrating one's place in the pecking order and incidentally hitting small balls into tiny holes.

There were other oddities about the golfers, like how the men dressed. Caucasian men (as far as I knew, all members were white) generally dressed in dull or dark colors, except on the golf course. Here they could wear pastel shades of blue, pink, and yellow with bright red pants, breaking away from the restrictiveness of traditional male dress in the workplace. Strangely, they flaunted their plumage not for women, but for each other; it was considered a kind of hyper-masculine display of their comfort with wealth and privilege.

ALTHOUGH CADDYING FELT LIKE BEING A GUN BEARER AT A SKEET SHOOT ON A COUNTRY ESTATE, IT WAS GOOD MONEY.

There were three classes on the golf course. On top were the golfers, then the caddies (many who would go on to college and one day evolve into golfers themselves), then the lifers who ran the caddy shack. (I suppose if you counted the kitchen workers, there were four classes, but I didn't interact with them.) Though technically "third class," the guys who managed the caddy shack wore their class as a badge of honor, as if everyone knew they were more masculine than their brightly bedecked masters. They were not unlike the lifers—Neil, Albert, and Charlie—I had met at Miami Bakery. Our two primary caddy masters both had names derived from colors. Whitey was short and wiry with a shock of blond hair, and Brownie was fat and scary, though not all that brown, being Caucasian.

Some of my friends from Brother Rice High School worked as caddies at the same club and there was a kind of camaraderie among us. Though we were all in the "going to college" class, Greg taught us to call ourselves slaves and decided we needed a secret sign to acknowledge each other on the golf course—something akin to hobo graffiti, only gestural in nature—because it was frowned upon to address a fellow worker while on the course. **So, Greg invented a simple, but subtle, greeting we could perform discreetly while passing each other.**

You brought your palm to the side of your torso then trailed it to the top of your head, like you were going to scratch your scalp (who could begrudge you a scratch?), and then, very quickly, you flashed an upright palm like a deer's white tail toward your friend. He would do the ritual gesture in response. These successful secret waves bonded us.

WE SINCERELY BELIEVED WE HAD FOOLED THEM.

CHAPTER 6
MONA FILMS

I'm not completely sure where Greg and I got the idea to become filmmakers. I think it had something to do with our high school English class taught by a rogue Christian Brother of Ireland, Brother Kovalesky. Somehow, he had the chutzpah and wherewithal to show us Bergman's *Wild Strawberries* during class. Given the ease of seeing films today, it's hard to imagine what this man had to go through to show us that movie. I don't think you could get films from libraries. First he had to find it, then find money to rent it. Next, a big metal canister containing the 16mm film would be mailed to the school. Then, he had to have the right kind of projector, given there were several sound technologies in use.

Surely, he was vulnerable to questions about the expense and appropriateness of his choice. And then he had to explain to a class of young jocks (whose ideas of radical art were the quick scene changes on *Laugh In*) why we were about to watch a movie in Swedish with English subtitles about death and strawberries.

Wild Strawberries did something to me, especially the dream sequence, where the main character sees a casket fly out of a horse-drawn carriage and open up at his feet, revealing a dead man with his own face.

SOMEHOW ANDY WARHOL CAME INTO THE MIX.

Greg was determined not to be limited by our suburban Catholic ghetto mentality. I'm not sure how he learned things—there was undoubtedly some coverage of the painter's antics on the news, but it would have been brief. We had no internet, no "underground newspapers," no alternative media of any sort, other than the Michigan Movin' radio show that played the wild-eyed radicals Peter, Paul and Mary once a week. Oh, and there was The Raven, a beatnik bar where you could listen to live folk music.

Somehow, Greg and I convinced our parents we needed to go to New York City to "check out the competition." I'm not sure if it was permissiveness, neglect, or just being caught by surprise that prevented them from stopping us. It helped that we had our own money from working, so we weren't asking them for anything but permission. I can't remember the sequence exactly, but we found a small theater on the campus of

Wayne State University in Detroit that showed "experimental films." One that impressed me was Ed Emshwiller's *Thanatopsis*, which was full of surreal imagery.

I still find it a bit hard to believe that two seventeen-year-old boys flew to New York in 1967 (probably my first airplane trip) and checked into a third-rate sleazy hotel near Times Square. *The Village Voice* told us where to find Warhol films, so there we went. We watched a few of the shorter ones but were unimpressed by his aesthetic of making his bourgeois audience uncomfortable in various ways. I think we walked out of *Sleep*, a five-hour yawn of a guy sleeping.

As we strolled out of the theater, Greg turned to me and said, "If this is the competition, we're not gonna make it." We went back to Michigan and launched the Mona Films, Ltd. Company. We even made ourselves business cards with a rooster for our logo. (It was never clear as to why we chose a rooster, though a chicken played an important role in one of our masterpieces.)

There was a rather strange kid at our school who was completely bald, probably from some medical condition no one bothered to ask him about. He wore a cheap red wig to school, but the back was stiff and you could easily see he had no hair underneath. When we learned his dad had an 8mm camera, Greg gave him the title of cinematographer to secure use of his equipment.

I should mention that my dad had a 16mm camera, but it had a non-adjustable focus and needed tons of light to get an image onto film. That's why so many of our family movies look like we're being scourged by a death ray as the line of four hot spotlights attached to a bracket panned us. So maybe my dad deserves some credit here that he could make movies, though his were strictly records of Christmas morning and other select family outings.

Greg and I fleshed out the plot to our first movie, *King Charlatan's Game*, in one afternoon and then faced casting. As the script called for Victorian whores, we naturally turned to our sister school, Marian High. We approached some of the girls our age with wilder reputations and found them willing. **Ahhh . . . Catholic girls.**

Location was the next problem. In the exurbs of Detroit, subdivisions butted up against working farms. We found one with significant acreage, combining stands of trees with fields of tall, waving grass. Most importantly, it had a scalable fence. It seems absurd now that we assumed we could film a movie on someone's property without even asking. But we did and never got caught.

I played the lead role of King Charlatan, while Greg volunteered himself and his brother Mark to play "the idiot twins," who wore creepy see-through masks and white uniforms we stole from the bakery. **They had the compelling role of stumbling around holding hands without any purpose.**

The plot involved a sexual encounter in the tall grass between the king and one of the harlots dressed in a Victorian gown. I think we had seen the Danish movie *Elvira Madigan* and ripped off the idea of the love scene from it. Our whores lived in a magical-realist forest grotto with a few pieces of furniture, including a birdcage hanging from a tree limb. The storyline called for Charlatan's lover to betray him and convince her two strumpet buddies to hunt him down and beat him to death with a stick, presumably for rape—a scene that required smearing my body with ketchup and filming it in slow motion.

We gathered a decent audience for the opening at the tony Birmingham Community Center. Determined to face potential critics face-on, Greg read a manifesto of sorts claiming *King Charlatan's Game* was "filmic synesthesia," a new kind of cinema. We showed the short movie in silence because we didn't know how to get music on 8mm film. It was a long fifteen minutes. At the end, people clapped and no one confronted us in outrage. The local paper, *The Birmingham Eccentric,* wrote an article entitled, "Teens Show Movie at Community Center."

WE WERE ON OUR WAY.

We immediately began planning our second film, *Nobody's Lost Willie.* Though I had no theatrical training whatsoever, I was again to star—as Willie. Greg recruited his mother to play the Mad Woman In The Woods, and this time we used my dad's ancient fixed-focus 16mm camera to film it. We were determined to have a film score, so we hired a budding folk talent from Marian High School to compose and sing an original song, also titled *Nobody's Lost Willie*.

We filled out the rest of the soundtrack with a poorly dubbed diatribe against commercial culture, performed on monkey bars with Greg and I forget who else. We plugged in various Vivaldi pieces for the rest of the film. And there was a chicken—a symbolic white chicken!—that Willie chased into Lake Michigan on location at Sleeping Bear Sand Dunes, near Traverse City.

We never made the third film, which Greg had entitled *Sylvia Zylantis*. It was supposed to be a campy take on a Wonder Woman concept. Instead, Greg and I went away to different colleges . . .

AND MONA FILMS FADED INTO MEMORY.

CHAPTER 7
DAIRY FACTORY

Borden's Dairy was the first job I had that an adult could do for their whole life. This was the kind of factory job where, if you didn't do anything awful, you could ride it to retirement. Like the bakery, we wore company-issued white uniforms. Probably because of a union, there was a high hourly wage that even the temporary workers received. **The entire Detroit area used to be like that: well-paid unionized workers who could afford a boat.**

At one time, Borden's was the largest producer of dairy products in the United States. Their logo was a happy cow named Elsie bedecked with a garland of daisies, like she was ready to be sacrificed in Sommerfest. She smiled her anthropomorphic smile at us from a huge wall mural. Not unlike Disney family trees, Elsie was part of a family headed by patriarch Elmer, who still has his picture on Elmer's glue. It is the one surviving product of the company's later bankruptcy.

My first job was working the night shift, 4–11 PM. I was "on the line," which meant putting gallon-sized plastic bottles onto a moving conveyor belt. The squarish bottles snaked along a metal track, disappearing into an opening, where I assumed they were filled with some liquid, most likely milk.

I worked at a station by myself. During breaks, there was some minimal communication with others working near me, mostly college kids on summer vacation. After some practice, I could lift four of the slippery containers at once and place them on the belt with one smooth motion. Any variation from the correct amount of pressure could cause the bottles to slip into an upward arc, catapulting each one in a different direction.

ONE OF THE OLD HANDS EVENTUALLY TRUSTED ME WITH A TECHNIQUE FOR MESSING UP THE LINE WITHOUT GETTING CAUGHT, THUS GIVING US EXTRA BREAK TIME.

The trick was to give the last bottle a strong shove, crushing a jug somewhere inside the filling machine. While the engineers tried to figure out what went wrong, we stood around feeling smug for sticking it to The Man.

I'm not sure I did anything to earn it, but I was offered a job working in the dairy laboratory. This job involved learning multiple procedures, and there were things you could do wrong that had more serious implications than a crushed plastic container jamming a machine.

The lab staff consisted of two kindly older guys and me. One of the tasks was to test cottage cheese to see how many days it took to go bad. We would dribble a bit of cheese into a petri dish and leave it unrefrigerated to grow critters. The fastest way to test a large number of samples was to line them up and pop the lids off in one gesture, moving the dish up to your nose for a quick sniff. When the samples went bad, it was usually sudden with little visual evidence, but the pungent aroma hit your nose with an intensity that made your whole body recoil in disgust.

I ended up working the lab the summer after freshman year at the University of Michigan and again the summer of sophomore year. Until I quit and moved to Colorado . . .

TO BE A HIPPIE.

CHAPTER 8
UNDERGROUND FILMMAKER

Freshman year at the Residential College at the University of Michigan, I made films with my girlfriend, Peggy. The idea of the college was to attend classes with the people in East Quad, a noble attempt to simulate a community of a small liberal arts college, like Bard, within the massive state institution. The admission staff relied on the Minnesota Multi-Phasic Personality test, where one of the questions was, "Do you like carrots cooked or raw?" So, we used Peggy's Super 8 camera and made a comedy film called *The Carrot Test*. Our idea was to parody the extensive testing the Rez-Coll did to select its applicants. Our hero was a scruffy proto-hippie with a biker 'stache who ended up spinning in a dryer, having been driven insane by the testing. **Deep stuff.**

Peggy and I had a competitor, a guy from Chicago named David Daskovsky. David was the kind of fellow who quoted Nietzsche at community meetings with a pretentious Chicago accent that sounded like it had a touch of London in it. Being an indie auteur, he was working on a piece modestly called *Opus*, which I can't remember ever seeing, though he talked about it a great deal. I assumed it would be Bergman to our bad Monty Python, and I was jealous of the serious aura he emanated.

The college invited poets and writers to do readings in our lounges. This was where I first met Michael, who became an important person in my life. I was immediately taken with his prose poems that spanned many subjects I had never taken seriously, let alone blended together into art. His sentences were full of science imagery (biology, astronomy, anthropology), occult references (Crowley and the Golden Dawn, astrology, tarot), and offbeat stuff like UFOs and science fiction. I talked to him afterward and told him my girlfriend and I were interested in filmmaking.

As it turned out so was he, and he invited us to his house. As a grad student in anthropology, he wasn't much older than me, but because he was married and lived in a real apartment off campus he seemed like an adult, something I could barely see in the hazy distance. Michael and his poet wife were affiliated with a group of artists and intellectuals descended from Black Mountain College.

Black Mountain, for a relatively brief time, was internationally famous for bringing artists together from various fields, a kind of North Carolina Bauhaus. The major poets were Robert Duncan, Robert Kelly, and Charles Olson. Olson had written a manifesto on "projective verse," which he put up as the antidote to "academic poetry" from the likes of Donald Hall and Robert Lowell. It was never entirely clear to me how one defined the "good" projective people from the "bad" academic people, but in a nutshell, these folks were closer to hippie intellectuals advocating freedom and cross-pollination. They made their "enemies" out to be formalists, like classical musicians who revered past masters at the expense of their own creativity.

I ADMIT, SOME OF THE "GOOD VS BAD" WAS HARD TO UNDERSTAND.

For example, they wholeheartedly embraced "experimental film," from Stan Brakhage to Ed Emshwiller, but didn't care for New Wave European film. They liked *some* of the Beats, like Gary Snyder, but disliked others, such as Allen Ginsberg. They built a lineage around Gertrude Stein and Ezra Pound, but weren't fond of the "confessional poets," like Sylvia Plath and Anne Sexton.

What I did figure out was that Michael was willing to mentor me in all of this, specifically focusing on the "underground film" movement. It probably wasn't as challenging as Brother Kovalesky showing *Wild Strawberries*, but Michael wrangled funds from his department to run an "anthropology film series" at the Residential College. Often, we would have tiny audiences watching the work of Brakhage, Maya Deren, Kenneth Anger, Bruce Conner, and Harry Smith, but some of the anti-establishment auteurs, like Andy Warhol and Jack Smith, didn't make the cut, again for somewhat obscure Black Mountain reasons.

When my freshman year ended, I bought an Agfa 8mm movie camera and began making films in my parents' basement. Since Michael and his wife lived only an hour away in Ann Arbor, I would drive to their house and show them my movies. Their encouragement and sense that there was a group of underground artists who would be interested in what I was doing was heady stuff. My films were mostly cut-out, frame-by-frame animations, a style not terribly unlike what South Park still uses, but I also did free-motion camera work like Brakhage, all intercut and nonlinear.

Sophomore year I met a young hippie girl named Judith, fresh from a mountain commune in Aspen. Peggy had given a recruitment talk at Highland Park High that Judith attended, and Peggy had invited her to the Rez-Coll where everyone was making films.

Judith and I had flirted a bit when I wrangled a slot as "guest artist" at her class on Gertrude Stein, taught by a fast-talking woman with fuzzy hair named Betsy Smith. Gertrude was famous for advocating repetition ("that's where people tell you what is important," she said). So, I filmed my sister Mary Anne in grainy black and white, repeatedly getting out of an overstuffed chair in my parents' living room and walking toward the camera. Judith was impressed. Her interest in studying "Poetry and Its Relation to the Universe" intrigued me, and soon enough, Peggy and I broke up and Judith and I became a couple.

Michael had since moved to Maine and I wanted to introduce him to Judith to get his blessing, in a sense. So we schlepped to Mount Desert Island for Thanksgiving, 1969, which wasn't easy since we didn't have a car or money.

UNFORTUNATELY, IT DIDN'T GO ALL THAT WELL.

Not only were we allergic to their cats, but Michael and his girlfriend suspected Judith was a "hippie" (oddly, a demerit to them at the time) and liked the "wrong artists." I never quite understood why they were so exclusionary and judgmental. After we left, my connection to Michael diminished into handwritten correspondence, while Judith and I plotted to become "real hippies."

THIS PROMPTED DROPPING OUT OF COLLEGE AND MOVING TO COLORADO.

CHAPTER 9
NUDE MODEL

Judith and I ended up in Colorado Springs where she was in a summer dance program taught by the prestigious Hanya Holm. While I had saved some money working a month or two at Borden's Dairy, we didn't have a source of income other than what her parents had given her for her summer program. So, Judith got a job modeling for an art class and then talked them into taking both of us. **Who wouldn't want to draw a young, naked hippie couple?**

As any art student can tell you, lifedrawing class is not nearly as sexy as it sounds to those who've never experienced it. In fact, it's quite the opposite. It was a hippie principle that breaking down the inhibitions of bourgeois society was a hurdle one could and should get over (not unlike believing in democratic socialism today). So we were supposed to think nakedness was "no big deal," and how better to prove it than nude modeling? This was a badge proving we were living beyond the Catholic and Jewish worlds we grew up in.

SO WE TOOK OFF OUR CLOTHES AND CLIMBED ONTO A RAISED PLATFORM IN THE MIDDLE OF A BUNCH OF KIDS WITH SKETCHPADS.

The teacher timed the poses with a stopwatch and would command "Change" every so many minutes. We struck improvisational poses inspired by Judith's dance classes, ending with a final pose that lasted fifteen minutes. It was all very professional.

I CONTINUED TO MAKE MY MOVIES, CORRESPOND WITH MICHAEL, AND READ FROM HIS RECOMMENDED LIST.

CHAPTER 10
DISHWASHER

As autumn approached, our summer school lifestyle had to change. First, we had to face the question of where to live. Colorado Springs was a conservative military town where our beloved counter-culture was barely present. Boulder to the north was the cool place to live, but we had no reason to settle there other than it was friendly to hippies.

Michael arranged for us to meet his brother, Thomas, who lived there with his austere girlfriend Martha. Judith called her an "herb girl." The Carlos Castaneda (*The Teachings of Don Juan: A Yaqui Way of Knowledge*) craze was in high gear. Everyone was reading his book and trying to enter a mystical zone with the help of hallucinogens, where one might see witches and demons. Thomas was taking it all very seriously and showed us a way of moving his eyeballs back and forth rapidly that helped him "see" visions. Though Thomas was a gracious enough host, there was nothing in Boulder to keep us there.

Judith had become serious about being a modern dancer, and her teacher, Hanya Holm, gave her a list of places in the US where one could study her preferred brand of German expressionist dance. I was still making my films and thought I could do that pretty much anywhere. In actuality, however, the list was short: Los Angeles, New York, Salt Lake City, and Minneapolis. We ruled out the two biggest cities right away, influenced by the anti-urban brand of hippie we espoused.

Salt Lake sounded spooky and cultish so that left Minneapolis. Since we had both grown up in the Midwest, we had some basic familiarity with what one might find in a city on the Great Plains, and the idea of moving to a completely unknown place was an adventure.

MINNEAPOLIS HAD A THRILLING RANDOMNESS TO IT, A PLACE KEROUAC AND HIS BUDDIES MIGHT MOVE TO IF THEY WANTED TO STUDY DANCE.

And so it was decided.

In the 1970s, Cedar Riverside was the Twin Cities' epicenter of hipness—a virtual

Haight-Ashbury. It had a candle store, a leather goods shop, a food co-op (still a new concept), and the city's primo vegetarian restaurant. There were also many bars with live music, though we were under the drinking age when we first moved there.

Right in the middle of it all was Mama Rosa's Italian Restaurant, a classic "red tablecloth" joint geared toward feeding parents who were visiting their offspring at the University of Minnesota. It also served an important function as the default employer for many of the newcomers.

Judith applied to be a waitress, but she was too young to serve beer and wine, so she had to settle for busgirl. I got a job as a dishwasher. Despite having experience cleaning racks at Miami Bakery, mozzarella cheese baked onto ceramic crockery was no joke. But I was glad to have a job and enjoyed the basic camaraderie amongst the staff that felt simultaneously subversive and inclusive. My main dishwasher buddy was another hippie who went by the name of Sheep, likely derived from his massive blond hair. **The cooks were older hippies who, for some reason, I imagined were practicing shamans in their off-hours.**

Judith planned to attend classes at the Nancy Hauser School of the Performing Arts on the West Bank of the Mississippi River. Before we got a real apartment, we lived in a downtown building, a hearty trek from the restaurant, that mainly housed immigrants from places like Somalia. Since Mama Rosa's didn't give us uniforms like the bakery, only aprons, walking home in winter piqued a vague Jack London-type of anxiety wondering . . .

HOW LONG WOULD IT TAKE TO DIE FROM FROSTBITE?

CHAPTER 11
HOSPITAL JANITOR

After we scored our coveted West Bank apartment and settled into the lifestyle of hippie artists, I wanted a job less frantic and transitional than Mama Rosa's. However, anything that required me to cut my shoulder-length hair or shave my scruffy beard was out of the question. Long hair on a male was a hard-won right, a sacred tribal emblem. There would be spiritual and emotional repercussions for compromising.

I heard a rumor that the big downtown hospital hired hippies. A county job was considered a good blue-collar gig, like being a postman. Apparently, the union rules banning discrimination (put in place for other reasons) ended up protecting the right of young men to wear their hair long. At the time, the hospital was simply called General Hospital, like the soap opera. Since I was looking for something part-time so I could continue making films during the week, I jumped at the opportunity to become a relief janitor on the weekends.

The uniform was a blue short-sleeved shirt with dark blue khaki trousers, not unlike the Catholic school uniforms I had worn for years. I didn't mind it, though. A uniform simplified the choice of what to wear to work. A few other young guys at the hospital, mostly orderlies, had long hair too. **We'd nod at each other as we passed in the hallways and exchange knowing looks that implied we all knew that after the revolution, we wouldn't need institutions like hospitals.**

As the weekend janitor, I could be assigned anywhere based on which janitors or maids were off duty. Thinking of myself as some kind of Jack Kerouac outsider with an affinity for the dark side, I had a secret preference for the most exotic locations, such as the Emer-gency Room and the Psych Ward.

HAVING ACCESS TO SUCH MYTHICAL PLACES WAS AN UNEXPECTED PERK.

On trash duty, I pushed a two-wheeled vehicle the size of a golf cart through the various buildings. When I went into the Psych Ward, patients regularly whispered requests for me to hide them in my cart and take them to freedom. I was flattered at the thought I might be this adventurous and generous to strangers, but still I wasn't tempted.

One time a particularly eccentric patient approached me as I made my way toward the locked door. He was a muscular vet with a thousand-mile stare, but not much older than me. His head was shaved in a style that hadn't become acceptable yet, adding to his crazed appearance. He would stand in the day room (which looked surprisingly similar to the setting in *One Flew Over the Cuckoo's Nest*) and adopt catatonic poses with his limbs rigid, like someone playing Christ in an experimental theater performance.

On that day, as I passed by with my oversized cart, he broke out of his frozen pose and grabbed the back of my shirt with a clenched fist. **When I turned and saw his wide eyes boring into me, he said, "I'll follow you wherever you go."**

His grip was so strong it took several orderlies to unclasp his hand from my shirt. As they did, strange as it sounds in the hubbub of that moment, I couldn't help but think how this would make a good story. But there was something about the words he chose that was haunting, so I erred on the side of caution and kept the encounter to myself so as not to stir up attention if he ever did get out.

I worked this job for several years, taking the bus to work before the sun rose. By today's standards, it's amazing that I could make enough to live on working only two days a week. But this job brought a stability to my life, not to mention . . .

IT GAVE ME TIME TO WORK ON MOVIES AND BE A HIPPIE.

CHAPTER 12
UNDERGROUND FILMMAKER II

Upon arriving in Minneapolis, I had every intention of working on my small films, even if it might not be related to a "career." I could see there was no viable bridge between these short film poems (à la Stan Brakhage) and any kind of livelihood. Plus, Michael had put forth his model for the "rebel intellectual": get a job in academia, preferably in a social science like anthropology or geography, and have a lively salon life on the side. This was what Robert Kelly did at Bard, and what Michael was doing at Hampshire College in Massachusetts. Michael believed English departments were corrupted by academic poetry and that film departments were blinded to seeing Bergman and Godard as the edge of experimentation. In his view, this kind of "narrative" storytelling, at least in film, was a thing of the past.

Having dropped out of the University of Michigan after sophomore year to go to Colorado, I still harbored a notion of getting a degree. Maybe it was my college-prep high school combined with Michael's idea of how to make a living. Partly because I was losing touch with him, I wondered if a film department at an art school might be a feasible choice. This idea sent me on a trip to visit the mildly famous filmmaker George Landow at the Chicago Institute of Art. I showed my films to Landow and another filmmaker, John Schofield, who was the straighter and more administrative of the two.

I was aware of Landow from seeing his short, quirky films at the Walker Art Center. He had a reputation as the preeminent trickster intellectual of underground cinema, and his works were thoughtful, playful, and generally questioned the "meta" nature of the film experience, particularly in his 1966 work, *Film in Which There Appear Edge Lettering, Sprocket Holes, Dirt Particles, Etc.*

In person, Landow was low-key and ironic, and somewhat less haughty than I expected. He had a coiffed "Jesus look" of the sophisticated urban hippie, while Schofield dressed preppy. Schofield, an administrator looking for talent as well as tuition, seemed to want to recruit me for the school. After I showed them my films and was alone with Landow, he confided, **"You're already making films, so why come here? We have nothing to teach you."**

IN A SENSE, THIS WAS WHAT I WANTED TO HEAR.

The truth was, I didn't really want to move to Chicago and go to film school. It would require tuition and the disruption of my living arrangement with Judith. So, I decided to go the "Michael track" and finish my BA at the University of Minnesota, majoring in geography, one of the less corrupted fields, in his opinion. I still wasn't sold entirely on the idea of life in academia versus a freelance life like Stan Brakhage had, but there was some comfort in settling in for two years of classes while I supported myself as a janitor.

In a sense, I was lucky that the university was experimenting with expanding the idea of geography beyond the traditional. I took a class from the somewhat famous, off-beat geographer, Yi Fu Tuan, who taught classes like Perceptual Space. I also studied historical geography and wrote a paper on the utopian communes of the 1840s.

As I continued working in my "underground film" niche, I began to wonder how I would ever get my work out into the world. It appeared I would need more money than I was making working two days a week as a janitor. To be a "real" filmmaker, I would need, minimally, to have 16mm prints (not 8mm or Super 8) to send to film festivals—and I would likely have to add sound. How could I afford any of that?

Simultaneously, I was becoming disillusioned with the hippie world, which seemed to be concretizing into a staid Eastern European style of East German socialism. **You worked at the co-op for your food discounts and you kept your head down and waited for the revolution.**

At 23, I needed a change. So, I cut my hair, broke up with Judith, and moved back to Detroit. Shockingly, this seemed like the easiest way to get a "real job," meaning I'd have access to my parents' "network" and also to their car. I think the radicalness of the idea appealed to me in a David Bowie-inspired...

CONCEPT OF SELF-REINVENTION.

CHAPTER 13
COMMERCIAL FILM

My parents were a bit baffled when I turned up in Detroit with short hair and a suspiciously new attitude. They had more or less written me off, figuring I was fully ensconced in living my life as a hippie. Nevertheless, they rallied when any of their children showed an interest in rejoining society, as it were, and they graciously let me sleep in my old room and use their car to go on job interviews.

General Motors, Chrysler, and Ford were bellwether American corporations since before World War II. There was even a slogan: "As GM goes, so goes the nation." Detroit was a big deal in advertising up to this point, as portrayed in *Mad Men*, but just as I was gearing up to push my "bright, creative, twenty-something" campaign on Detroit's massive industrial infrastructure, the oil crisis of 1973 hit. OPEC (Organization of the Petroleum Exporting Countries) placed an oil embargo on the US, pissed we were not stepping aside and allowing them to destroy Israel. Gas prices shot from 39 cents a gallon to $2.53 in one year—and that's in 1973 dollars. The equivalent move in 2020 dollars would be from $2.28 per gallon to almost fifteen!

As a result, things changed overnight for Motown. The consumer market turned on a dime away from its love of "muscle cars" toward buying the smaller, cheaper Japanese models that auto execs had recently chuckled about during their three-martini lunches.

Consumers, and the people who made things to consume, went into full panic mode. By 1975, Toyotas would outsell Volkswagens—the "fun import" of the earlier decade. Despite the gods raining on my one-man parade, I had no choice but to forge ahead with my plan to sneak in the back door of the once-prosperous local economy.

AS IT TURNED OUT, MY DAD WASN'T MUCH OF AN INDUSTRIAL NETWORKER.

He did set me up with one "informational interview" at Federal Mogul (who the hell knew what they made), but all I got from it was, "Hang in there, kid."

There was one man in corporate advertising who lived in our little Catholic subdivision of

Greenwich Green. He had a reputation as a drunk and seemed to be coasting toward retirement at McCann-Erickson, a high-profile agency. In preparation for an after-work meeting in his living room, I mocked up a breakfast cereal box and animated a commercial with a claymation horse.

My naiveté and optimism about that day are painful to look back on, even after all these years. While my recollection of the ordeal is spotty, I do remember him clinking the ice in his drink as he thoroughly discouraged me from pursuing anything even close to advertising. Agencies, he said, were laying off en masse due to the oil embargo. I didn't even show him the pathetic improvisations I had brought along to show off my multifarious creative skills.

Somehow, I found a Detroit-area filmmaker named David Hilton, who was scraping a living together doing gigs for the auto companies. He was nice enough and was impressed by my thwarted attempt at becoming a full-time underground filmmaker. He couldn't offer me much encouragement, but he hired me as a grip for an industrial shoot, where I helped someone dress a set for a "typical American garage." Meanwhile, I kept sending out resumes to anyone in the Yellow Pages who called themselves a commercial film studio.

Even before the oil crisis, Detroit's home-grown commercial film industry was fading. Its flagship agency was named Jam Handy, and they made good-citizenship shorts on top of ads for cars, such as *Hired!* (1940) and *A Case of Spring Fever* (1940), that were featured on *Mystery Science Theater 3000* for humor.

One exception to the decline of the commercial film industry was the White Association, unironically run by African-American Mr. White. White maneuvered his status as a minority-owned business to stay afloat in the first blush of corporate affirmative action, despite the fact that everyone in the shop besides him was Caucasian.

Mr. White lived in a mansion on Grand Boulevard, where General Motors executives had built homes in a neighborhood with a storied past to be close to the company headquarters. Mr. White hired me as a lowly gopher, which meant driving stuff to and from the set for minimum wage using my parents' car. For some reason I couldn't quite figure out, he never liked me.

Getting my "foot in the door" of a dying industry was nothing to get excited about. It reminded me vaguely of my job as a caddy, and at this subsistence level of income, there was no way I could launch my departure from my parents' home in the affluent suburb of Bloomfield Hills. After a few tepid months of feeling underappreciated and underutilized, I became discouraged.

I WANTED A REAL JOB, AND I KNEW THIS WASN'T IT.

CHAPTER 13
IMPC ORDER CLERK

I started scouring newspaper ads for jobs, any kind of job, and found one that looked promising and quirky—a night clerk supervisor at a precious metals sales company. The location was oddly in spitting distance from my dad's office at Northland, which happened to be the largest mall in the world in 1948. International Precious Metals Corporation, or IPMC, was a subsidiary of MultiVest, a local real estate developer that had leased enough floors in a ten-story office building to put their name on it.

I did own a typewriter, but for some reason I now cannot fathom, I didn't even make the modest effort of retyping my resume. **It was standard practice to tailor one's resume to reflect that the job you were interviewing for was your dream job.** I could have at least put my career goal as: "to work in the field of metals and investment," but I suspect I had some kind of reluctance to put such a lie in writing.

Normally, this attitude doesn't get you very far in job interviews, but this one was different because the man who interviewed me, Perry Peterson, was sort of a closet hippie. Though he was an engineer by training, I learned Perry was recruited to run IPMC by a college friend (Ivy League, no doubt), perhaps because Perry fully looked the role of a young executive of the '70s. He sported his hair longish, had a Burt Reynolds mustache, and wore a crisp suit wide in the shoulders. He seemed even cooler to me when I found out his girlfriend had worked with Koko, the famous ASL-signing gorilla at the San Francisco Zoo.

What made the encounter with Perry truly eccentric—and landed me the job—was my handwriting. Perry was a believer in the quasi-science of graphology, or handwriting analysis. At its most basic, he believed clear handwriting meant a person thought in orderly ways. He asked me to write something, and thanks to the Sisters of Charity at Our Lady Queen of Martyrs, I had excellent penmanship. I knew I had made a good impression when Perry said, "Is that your real handwriting?" Despite my slacker resume, I got the job.

THOUGH THE SALARY WAS NOT OUT OF LINE FOR AN

OFFICE JOB, IT WAS MORE MONEY THAN I HAD EVER MADE BEFORE.

MultiVest was positioning IPMC to become an international sales operation where reps could place orders from any time zone 24/7, and I was the sole "night clerk supervisor."

Alone in this huge office from roughly four PM to midnight, with relatively little to do, it wasn't long before Perry realized I might be more useful on the day shift to help supervise a growing population of order clerks. Our clerks were young, attractive women who recorded our sales reps' orders and walked them over to the "trading desk" to be logged. From their cubicles, the reps would flirt with the girls as they handed their work through a bank teller opening in the glass.

We sold silver, gold, copper, and gold coins. Perhaps trying to make it feel more like a real trading room, Perry had the order clerks yell out how many ounces of which metal they were buying from a posted price that was constantly changing with the market. Our "trader," a young Economics major named Denise, would cover our sales by buying commodity contracts on the metals exchanges in New York. **With all the yelling and high energy, it was an exciting environment to work in.**

Influenced by an apocalyptic theorist named Harry Browne (*How to Profit from the Coming Devaluation,* 1970), our boss, Marty Rom, imagined the price of silver (the number two precious metal) was poised for a meteoric rise.

When people are thinking doomsday, they traditionally turn to precious metals as a store of value. But in reality, precious metal prices always fluctuate, reacting to supply and demand as well as economic news. The prices tended to rise on "bad news" and decline with "good news," but discoveries of ore or sudden shifts in international attitudes could also affect them. In this case, the volatility of the silver price caught everyone off guard who bought into Harry Browne's ideas.

Somewhat surreptitiously to the uninformed, we were selling silver on margin, which means the company loaned the buyer the bulk of the value of the contract to leverage a bigger win. We were on margin with our brokers as well, so when the market price fell too far, our clients would owe us more money to stay in the game.

THIS WAS CALLED "MARGIN CALL," AND MOST OF THEM NEVER REALIZED THIS COULD HAPPEN.

Theoretically, the margin calls were between the reps and their clients, but because it happened during a crisis, our clerks had to field angry calls from people who were threatened with being "sold out" by our reps. This meant that if they didn't put in more money, they would be sold out at a loss once our fees were subtracted.

EVEN THESE CRISES DIDN'T STOP THE BUSINESS FROM GROWING, AND LUCKILY, I EXCELLED.

CHAPTER 15
PRECIOUS METALS TRADER

It wasn't long before Perry added a trading component to the supervisory aspects of my job, which entailed assisting Denise in placing orders for the commodity contracts. Unfortunately, I wasn't a numbers guy and made a lot of mistakes until I learned to check my figures more than once. This meant that Denise, who was intelligent and attractive with long blond hair, got a lot of practice shaking her mane like a horse's tail when she was mad at me.

Both Denise and I placed commodity orders ("futures") through our brokers to cover the amount of metal-on-paper we sold on leverage. One of the fun aspects was to try to "beat the market" by replenishing inventory at prices lower than what we sold them. This is how we locked in a "trading profit," which was gravy for IPMC. **At first, it was surprisingly difficult just understanding the brokers when they talked.** The combination of heavy New York accents and rapid-fire speech, filled with trading jargon and insider shorthand, was akin to listening to an unusual dialect like Scottish Glaswegian.

As I got used to it, I enjoyed the brokers' fascinating tales of how a new copper find in Chile or a mining strike in South Africa would affect the metal's price at the open. They explained how government announcements on "the money supply" could encourage the market to go up or down. Traditionally, precious metal prices went up when the news was bad, but copper was still mostly an industrial metal so it didn't react the same as others. Perry had a pet theory that pennies were going to become obsolete because they contained more copper than a cent was worth, so he bought a vast hoard of uncirculated pennies. (I never found out if that was folly or not.)

IT'S NOT IMPOSSIBLE THAT I COULD HAVE REMAINED AT IPMC, POSSIBLY FOR YEARS.

If I had stuck around, I might have found a niche in the metals investment industry. But I chose to leave for two somewhat related reasons. First, Judith and I decided to get married. She had moved to New York City at this point and had a job with the prestigious Trisha Brown Dance Company. My goal in coming back to Detroit was to get a real job and I had accomplished that, but I didn't know if my resume was enough to land me a metals job in New York.

Second, while the IPMC model wasn't a scam, it walked dangerously close, like a late-night infomercial. People were buying our precious metals as a hedge against inflation, while inadvertently taking out a loan on a volatile commodity they knew nothing about. Many didn't have any back-up cash for margin calls and lost everything they put in. Our company did not participate in these losses, but they did stand on the sidelines with a cleverly crafted win-win for themselves. **It was not unlike being a legal loan shark, presenting ourselves as a comfort to the worried, then stepping away when things went bad.** It was a world in which I didn't feel comfortable putting down roots.

The tough part was that the metals industry had afforded me newfound affluence. Now that I had left hippie scarcity behind—no more schlepping groceries in a backpack through the snow, among other unpleasantries—I had an apartment, my first car, and money in the bank. But if I was going to leave, I was determined that the work I had put in be parlayed into a step up the ladder of employment, meaning I needed to make my thin metals resume look like something more than a desperate first-rung job anyone could do. It was a daunting prospect.

HOW WOULD I START FROM SCRATCH IN THE BIG APPLE AS JUST ANOTHER DIME-A-DOZEN COLLEGE GRAD?

CHAPTER 16
SILVER TRADER NYC

Judith and I made a plan: I would try to get a job in New York from Detroit, then I would move and we would get married. Easier said than done.

The energy crisis was still going gangbusters and my affiliation with the metals industry was thin, at best. There was the additional problem of a potential employer possibly seeing IPMC more as an investment company than a metals trading company. Worse, if they looked into it, it might look more like a loan sharking infomercial that preyed on fear.

I hired a headhunter to find me a job. It wasn't a horrible idea, though my radar for sleazeballs had already proven a little bit faulty. The company I hired, Douma and Associates, turned out to be a borderline scam, claiming they had a process that "guaranteed" a job if you paid an exorbitant fee. Who guarantees anything where it actually pays off?

Surprisingly, they did get me a job, though being hired on probation by a firm with no "skin in the game" may not have been worth the cost. Nevertheless, it was a real metals company, evidenced by their name—Metal Traders—and the position was assistant to the silver trader.

With a grand send-off from family, friends, and IPMC, I was off to start a new life in the Big Apple. I moved into the apartment Judith found in Cobble Hill, and, as planned, we got married at her parents' condo by a Jewish judge on the 57th floor of the Ritz-Carlton Building in Chicago.

When I walked into Metal Traders Midtown Manhattan office on my first day and met the top boss, my gut tightened. Mr. Morosco was an oily-haired man with the shifty eyes of a mobster. He made Perry Petersen on his shiftiest day look like an Eagle Scout, which he probably had been. When Mr. Morosco introduced me to the head silver trader, my stomach clenched even more.

Kevin Shinners was a lean, sandy-haired man with a slight stoop due to the chip on his shoulder from not attending an Ivy League college. Kevin spoke in a heavy New York brogue, the kind they use in movies for cab drivers. I immediately judged him as one generation removed from the laborers who built the Brooklyn Bridge (and a guy to avoid on St. Paddy's Day). Despite sensing we would never achieve the slightest rapport, I dutifully went about my job recording what Kevin was doing.

The skinny Irish-American was constantly on the phone, snarling and swearing at some son-of-a-bitch floor broker. In order to record his trades, I was supposed to understand what was going on. Luckily, I knew a bit from IPMC. There would be a "bid" (the price at which someone wanted to buy) and an "ask" (what they were willing to sell for). I knew commodity silver traded as months into the future, and I knew about hedges and spreads—buying one month and selling another so that your position is neutral. Basically, no one really wanted to own anything. It was all about taking advantage of small differences in the numbers.

It was my job to know what spreads Kevin was working, and he would have several going at any given time. When a trade was complete, I had to write it up. The traders spoke in jargon and assumed their assistants mostly knew what they were "working" (in months, quantities, and prices), so they might only say the last two digits to indicate what was happening. Given the speed of things, there was an expectation that I could do quick adding and subtracting in my head—a skill they clearly didn't notice I'd left off my resume.

I KNEW FROM THE FIRST DAY I WAS NOT GOING TO BE A GOOD SILVER TRADER'S ASSISTANT, ESPECIALLY TO THIS KEVIN GUY.

None of the required skills overlapped anything I had done at IPMC, which started to feel like office management. What I quickly learned was this kind of trading was all about fast math you do in your head. The kind of market narratives my Detroit brokers used to enchant me with were not entirely irrelevant, but here they quickly translated into numbers.

My sense of being the incompetent new guy never wore off. I thought going out with the guys would help somehow—the trading day ended early and the men (the traders were all men) went out nearly every day for drinks. While most of the other guys weren't as socially challenged as Kevin, there didn't seem to be a way to parlay my assets into improving my situation. So, I dutifully complied with the serious drinking expected on these outings, looking to create some sort of bond that might make this job viable.

While I am generally quite tolerant of people, I loathed Kevin and felt it was mutual. At the time, I didn't peg his similarity with Charlie Nichols from the bakery, but he definitely had his sullen sense of imminent explosion.

About a month in, the brand-new head of the human resources department called me into her office and fired me. It was clumsy and shocking, made worse because it was done by a complete stranger. Somehow, I found the *chutzpah* to request a face-to-face with two colleagues I knew. Perhaps it was an attempt to save face, or perhaps I just needed time to let it sink in that months of prep (let alone the fee I paid the headhunter) was a complete failure.

I only vaguely remember the conversations with my colleagues. I'm sure I tried hard to look calm and attentive, as someone wanting to learn from the experience, but my mind was screaming. I was too green when I walked out to even need that box you see laid-off people carry out in movies, full of family photos and a pathetic plant.

With only my briefcase in hand, I felt weird walking out into Midtown Manhattan having just been fired.

> I DIDN'T KNOW WHAT TO DO, OTHER THAN WHAT I HAD SEEN TOUGH GUYS DO IN MOVIES WHEN SOMETHING HORRIBLE HAPPENED TO THEM.

I found a shot-and-a-beer place, ordered a scotch, and downed it like Jimmy Stewart trying to forget a giant rabbit was stalking him.

Telling Judith wasn't so hard. She was in a twelve-step program and had been upset by all the drinking, so there was some relief.

BUT BEING NEWLY MARRIED AND FIRED FOR INCOMPETENCY AFTER ALL THE EFFORT I HAD PUT IN WAS UNDENIABLY HUMILIATING.

CHAPTER 17
BUNKER HILL

I was afraid I had "blown" my resume in the metals industry, now that I had the IPMC problems and had been fired from my second metals job. Nevertheless, I persisted and managed to scrounge up a trickle of job leads for entry-level positions.

Soon, I got wind of a job I thought the gods had crafted specifically for me. Tennent Metals was an old-school trading firm that delivered real commodities to real end-users in the tradition of the great trading companies like Hudson's Bay and East India. They even had a training program! Unfortunately, fate teased me with this then failed to deliver.

LUCKILY, THE BUNKER HILL MINING COMPANY CAME ALONG AS MY SAVIOR.

The Bunker Hill Mine was first opened in 1887. They dug ore out of the ground in Idaho and smelted it into bars of silver, lead, and zinc. The ideal candidate needed to be organized and moderately good at communication, with down-to-earth office skills to keep track of sales. It seemed no "head math" was required, and they hired me. As soon as I started working at Bunker Hill in their offices overlooking St. Patrick's Cathedral in Midtown, my life began looking up.

The boss, David Bancel, was a kindhearted but nervous man with the demeanor of an English professor, and the top salesman was Bill Ridgway, a hard-driving dealmaker born of English ex-pats in Peru who spoke fluent Spanish and English with a British accent. Our receptionist was a beautiful African-American woman named Pat who dressed in African-inspired outfits involving exotic hairdos, enormous earrings, and bright prints. The other two young guys in the office were Ron—pure Ivy League Connecticut: tall, good-looking, and gentrified—and Jim, a slightly more civilized version of John Belushi. A second secretary named Kriste was a wan white girl from Long Island who wanted to be Joni Mitchell. Occasionally, she even brought her guitar to the office and sang original songs for the "guys." The lot of us were overseen by our president, a young cowboy who could have been a stand-in for Clint Eastwood.

I partnered over the phone with a savvy woman named Jan who worked at the headquarters in

Kellogg, Idaho. My main job was recording sales on a spreadsheet and making sure our numbers agreed with Idaho's. Jan became a trusted colleague, somewhat reminiscent of Denise at IPMC. We helped each other out and shared off-the-record gossip to enhance each other's positions. She also taught me about corporate politics, explaining that what the upper echelon wanted to hear was often different than reality. In other words, she had a knack of finding out what was "really going on" and letting me in on it.

My savvy skills led me, almost accidentally, into sales via customer service. A crabby customer would call with a complaint and demand to talk to the boss. I began to step up, asking them what was wrong and offering help. They might gripe about a late railcar, an inaccurate assay of our product, or a billing error. Before I knew it, several of these tough old birds would ask for me. Management noticed and I segued into being more of a customer service guy. While chatting with clients, it wasn't that difficult to talk them into taking another railcar of whatever metal they had contracted, and . . .

VOILÀ—I WAS A SALESMAN!

CHAPTER 18
SALESMAN TRAINEE

Once Bunker Hill officially made me a salesman, I began to travel with Bill. We flew all over the country, calling on buyers who were large enough to handle railcars of lead or zinc. Lead went to small battery manufacturers on the South Side of Chicago or in rural Pennsylvania, and to large ones like Rayovac with plush offices in downtown Philadelphia. Zinc was mainly used for die-casting parts and had a similar range, from the small operators in Los Angeles to General Motors.

Some customers were huge bureaucracies, but many were family-owned businesses of all types: Texans in cowboy hats, impeccably dressed New Yorkers, tough-talking Chicagoans, and friendly Los Angelenos who drove me around in a golf cart. I didn't need to know much about their businesses (batteries, steel, metal recycling, die-casting), but being a "generalist" and a good schmoozer was a definite asset.

We drank and ate, sometimes more drinking than eating. Occasionally, we talked about the metal market, but these guys already knew what we sold. Often it was about playing ourselves against other vendors, many with more modern facilities (and higher purities) than the ancient smelters of Bunker Hill. Soon, I began making more money and buying classy suits.

I FELT I COULD BREATHE A SIGH OF RELIEF: FOR THE FIRST TIME, JUDITH AND I HAD EXCESS CASH THAT WASN'T SOMEHOW CONNECTED TO HER FAMILY.

Every day, I took the subway from Brooklyn to my uptown office, wearing a suit and carrying a briefcase. I was well-liked and competent, and the company seemed stable and the business solid.

I HAD SUCCESSFULLY REINVENTED MYSELF.

CHAPTER 19
LEAD SMELTER

In 1977, when I was 27, the unions at Bunker Hill went on strike. Our cowboy president decided to keep the refining operations running by using white-collar workers. Somewhat symbolically, as the cost of flying us out and putting us up must have been more than what we offered in terms of physical work, he brought the New York sales team in to do our share. They let me bring Judith along as a sort of executive perk and put us up at a cutesy guest house in the mountains.

I felt odd leaving this swanky little cottage dressed like a smelter—protective overalls, thick gloves, hard hat, goggles, and rubberized boots with metal tips. It was one of the few times in my life I regretted we weren't into taking selfies. **Despite wondering how hard the work would actually be, I was excited to try my hand at the manly trade of being a smelter.**

I got a tour of the mine, descending into the shaft on a sledge (basically a flat piece of wood) at high speed, with a wall of rock whizzing past inches from my head. If you reached out a hand to touch it, you'd probably lose it. On the sledge, the men sat on benches facing each other with so little room that you had to put your knee into the crotch of the person across from you, with someone's knee in yours.

My job was in the silver smelter—an ancient factory with belching smoke and open-flame furnaces like something out of the 19th century, which it basically was. Silver bars were smelted in several stages. First, a front-end loader dumped about thirty cooling ingots resembling oversized loaves of bread onto the metal platform where I stood in rubber boots. As the platform started to warm up, I could feel the heat through the soles. I wondered if they gave the new guys these shoes to see how long would they would last before they complained.

UNLESS MY BOOTS MELTED, I WAS DETERMINED TO SUCK IT UP.

I had a hard time believing how primitive and labor-intensive this job was. The cooling silver bars weighed about seventy pounds each. We had to pick them up with our awkwardly gloved hands, then attempt to "toss" them into a fifteen-inch diameter hole of red-hot inferno. It was like a carnival game from hell.

I wasn't out of shape, but I wasn't a big guy either, and I had only been working for a few days when my first accident happened. One of my gloved fingers got trapped between the edge of the hole and the seventy-pound ingot. I didn't lose a finger, but I did need stitches. The hardest thing was graciously accepting the running joke that the New Yorker had managed to hurt himself on purpose to get out of work.

Thanks to my injury, Judith and I ended up having a vacation in the mountains while the rest of the white collars sweated it out in the smelter.

THE ENDURING JOKE FROM MY SHORT-LIVED STINT WAS THAT I HAD MESSED UP THE SAFETY RECORD BY BEING THE ONLY INDUSTRIAL ACCIDENT DURING THE STRIKE.

CHAPTER 20
MIDWEST REGIONAL MANAGER

At this point, my original boss in New York, David Bancel, had died and Bill had gone to work for a competitor. Our new boss, Gary Wickham, came from a different competitor (companies preyed on each other for employees). Gary and I got along fine, which was a relief. But the management decided they needed a Midwestern presence and proposed that I move and start an office there. The plan was to make me Midwest Sales Manager, Lead and Zinc Products.

Judith wasn't excited to move back to her hometown for a number of reasons. She never liked the city much and she had a lot of friction with her parents. She loved her job with the Trisha Brown Dance Company, and Chicago wasn't well known for dance, outside of one ballet company, which was irrelevant to her genre. And while she had considered her next step might be (in the distant future) quitting Trisha to do her own work, she had visualized this happening in the dance capital of the world, New York. **Nevertheless, we decided to move.**

We awaited the moving truck on a wintery day in February, with sleet making the streets icy. Bunker Hill was paying for everything, even packing up our house and putting my Karmann Ghia into the moving van. Brooklyn parking being as horrible as its reputation, I assumed a big-name moving company would know how to handle it, maybe with special permits or ways to clear a space. That is, until there was a knock at the door. It was the van guy standing there with a weird look on his face.

"WHERE DO I PARK?" HE ASKED.

My stomach clenched as I saw his massive van double-parked on the tiny street. Thankfully, the gods gave me a break and we miraculously managed a couple of spots for the van about a half block away. We watched as the crew packed our belongings and shuttled them down the icy streets, holding our breath each time. Luckily, the team and our belongings survived without incident.

Judith had previously gone to Chicago and found us a huge apartment (by New York standards) in the Loyola University area on the north side. Once we were settled, I rented a one-man office in the nearby suburb of Skokie, complete with the cutting-edge technology of a fax machine. I was only into my new job a few months when Gary called and told me management had decided to move the main sales office to Chicago, which meant I would be in charge of finding and furnishing our new office space. He wanted something luxurious and downtown, with an impressive address. **I was out of my depth navigating Chicago real estate and choosing furniture, but being trusted to do this was a kind of honor.**

Not long after, Judith and I were unceremoniously kicked out of our Rogers Park apartment when they decided to turn it into condos. It was a shock, but it gave us an opportunity to go Bohemian. Luckily, we knew what "key money" was—paying the exiting renters for their "fixtures" (kitchen, laundry, etc.)—from our time in New York. As a result, we scored a third story walk-up loft, complete with all the trimmings, within walking distance of the new Michigan Avenue offices.

Our hip living arrangement seemed to mitigate the impact of being a corporate guy, as most of our new friends would come from Judith's world of dancers and performance artists. At first, I was a bit uncomfortable being the only guy in our circle with a "straight job," but I had never given up my true passion:

I WAS STILL AN ARTIST.

CHAPTER 21
ZOOGRAPHICO PRESS

During the punk days of the late '70s and early '80s, a kind of do-it-yourself aesthetic arose, inspired by garage bands and street culture. The graphic novel was evolving out of the work of "underground cartoonists" like R. Crumb, Charles Burns, and Art Spiegelman (*Maus*, 1991), who were hitting the mainstream through magazine illustrations and album covers. Punk's eschewing of technique was a liberation for many artists. It inspired a kind of homemade comic called a *zine*, which began showing up on kiosks in record and clothing stores.

My desire to make a book of drawings had as much to do with *The New Yorker* artist, Saul Steinberg, as anything. The quirky surreal drawings of a successful cartoonist, unworried about how the world categorized him, was compelling.

Steinberg was best known for his *View from Ninth Avenue*, a cover that showed New York looking across a nearly empty Middle America, dotted with small cities like Chicago and abruptly ending at the Pacific Ocean. At the Residential College, a young woman from New York said my drawings reminded her of Steinberg, who I didn't know at the time. My first book, *January* is *Alien Registration Month*, was definitely influenced by him, though perhaps leaning a bit more abstract "conceptual." I got the title from late-night public service announcements stating, "January is alien registration month." This was before immigration became the heated issue it is today. I loved the extraterrestrial double entendre implied.

I called my company Zoographico Press, loosely inspired by reading about zoophilia in Kraft-Ebbing's Sexual Psychopathy in high school. How I got a hold of that book, I have no idea. While the zines relied on the liberating technology of the newfangled Xerox machines, they were still expensive by the page. The alternative was offset printing, where the setup costs include printing plates for large runs. (The page cost decreased by volume, but you had to have a certain minimum run to justify the expense.) My goal was to hold one of my own books in my hand, and since I was making money, I decided my "business self" could subsidize Zoographico.

Though I gave no thought to how I would actually sell them, having

the physical object in hand with a glossy cover, perfect binding, and a real ISBN hooked me on the phenomenon of making books.

My second book, *Nuclear Pup*, was inspired by underground cartoon characters. I presented the "plot" in one-panel vignettes with my star, *Nuclear Pup*, a harlequin Great Dane who morphed into an anthropomorphic form via radiation. I drew him in various situations, like a montage from the life of an undercover, time-traveling James Bondian hero. He was Elliot Ness in one, an Afghani freedom fighter in another, an undercover cross-dressing policeman in another.

My approach was meant to mess with the idea of a narrative character by casting him in endearing, slightly drug-addled situations without context. Perhaps neither narrative enough nor surreal enough, he never quite worked. **That didn't stop me, though.**

I had always gravitated to the side of a conflict I wasn't "supposed" to identify with. For example, I always wanted to be an Indian in Cowboys and Indians. When I got into building models, I made a Japanese Zero, the Battleship Yamato, and a Chinese junk. I remember being impressed by a scene in *King Richard and the Crusaders* (1954) where Saladin demonstrated how a Saracen blade could slice a silk scarf tossed in the air cleanly in half. (King Richard tried to duplicate the feat with his blunt but powerful sword to no avail.) Long before it was *de rigeur*, I wondered why the history of "non-Western" civilizations wasn't being taught to us. At the time, it seemed like I had discovered something. So, by the time I drew for my third book (after giving up on *One Hundred Alien Madonnas*), I decided to go even wilder. As a child, I found Genghis Khan fascinating, particularly how he had conquered the world's largest empire yet was barely mentioned in history books.

WHAT ELSE WEREN'T THEY TELLING US?

Another influence for *The Second Mongolian Invasion* was the punk music scene: Devo, the B-52s, the Talking Heads, X-Ray Spex, and perhaps even the Beat poet William Burroughs with his weird mix of paranoia, drug narratives, and science fiction. Merging my love of B movie science fiction with the Mongols, I created invaders from outer space defined by things I liked to draw. These included fedora hats, chakras, quirky architectural elements (pagodas and mosques), all jumbled together.

At some point, I received a morsel of recognition, almost by accident. I'm not even sure how they saw it, but *The Second Mongolian Invasion* was selected by Chicago's Museum of Contemporary Art for their Permanent Artist Books Collection. Whether they still have such a collection, I have no idea.

During the time I was creating my three Zoographico books, I also became a published cartoonist. *The Chicago Reader* was a free weekly publication with cartoons. They published Lynda Barry (who got moderately famous) and Matt Groening (who got super famous), as well others who never did. Ironic cartoon humor had already been mainstreamed by Bill Griffith's *Zippy the Pinhead*, B. Kliban's *Never Eat Anything Larger Than Your Head*, and Gary Larson's *The Far Side*. On a whim, I contributed *The Difference between a Punk and a Dork* to *The Reader*. My drawing depicted two guys who were quite similar, but with tiny differences pointed out by arrows so that readers could tell which was the cool one and which was to be disdained. It was a thrill to be published in a popular newspaper, and I enjoyed a short run with *The Reader* under the name C. B. Murphy.

EVENTUALLY, I HIT A BUMP.

The top dog at *The Reader* personally chose the cartoons, and at first, he accepted mine rather easily. Then, a few got rejected and I couldn't understand why. Other cartoons with a similar aesthetic seemed to be getting published more regularly, so I decided to visit him. We ended up discussing a particular cartoon of mine in classic back-and-forth fashion.

"It's not funny," he said.

"Yes, it is," I said.

As you might imagine, this was the making of a losing argument for me as the creator.

I LEARNED YOU CAN'T TALK SOMEONE, ESPECIALLY THE BOSS, INTO BELIEVING SOMETHING IS FUNNY WHEN THEY THINK IT'S NOT.

CHAPTER 22
THE GODFATHER

If the mob had made their living off bathroom accessories, Judith's family could have rivaled the Corleones from *The Godfather*. There was an Old World, Judeo-Russo charm about the clan, where men kissed on both cheeks and went to steam baths to discuss deals. Coming from the cynical Murphy clan, where a well-placed dagger of irony was the high bar of emotion, I was attracted to this uninhibited expression of both anger and love. **I understood I was an outsider and would always be the goy-in-law, but even the Corleones valued their non-Italian son.**

I had ended up in the metals business mostly by accident, where I clung to my resume, despite having no real interest in what I was doing. I would likely "climb the ladder," but I would always be in a marketing department of a large conglomerate, like the one that owned Bunker Hill. Though there was no reason that looked particularly worse than other options, I began to entertain the idea that joining my father-in-law Mike's business would solve several problems.

For starters, the family business—Selfix—was growing and had made Judith's parents wealthy. I got along fine with them, and from what I could tell, they liked me. Truth be told, I figured that Judith and I would eventually benefit from her family's assets, and it made sense to at least try to contribute energy to their business, which was manufacturing and importing household goods. While I didn't bring any technical skills or knowledge of manufacturing to the table, I rationalized this field would be easier to relate to than ingots of smelted metal, and I hoped my experience in sales and marketing could be beneficial after a brief apprenticeship. In short, I always counted on basic common sense going a long way. How hard would it be to become useful to a company with a completely different structure and product line in a totally different industry?

I THINK THE WORD IS HUBRIS.

The first time Mike asked me to join his company, I assumed he was joking. Whenever I'd told him stories about incompetent management at Bunker Hill, he would say, "They should make you president," but given what I knew about him, the job offer could have just been one more way the Frank Sinatra generation swaggered; they tended to offer things they never expected you to accept—a cheeky win-win for them. But knowing Mike wasn't a man who passed out compliments easily, I began to think his offer to join the family business might be real.

When I announced my intention to team up with her dad, Judith was not pleased. Being the only daughter in a patriarchal business family had been traumatic, especially when she rebelled against expectations of how women were supposed to act in this world. Her two older brothers had rejected working for the firm, another red flag I was oblivious to. One night while drinking in her parents' 52nd-floor condo above the Ritz-Carlton in Chicago, I took him by surprise by asking if his offer was real. **I suppose he could have backed out, but instead, he said yes.**

Though negotiations needed to take place, I felt I was making what could be a lifetime commitment—until Mike said I made too much money for the kind of job he could offer me. He explained that even if he brought me in as an assistant to the president (a weird title to begin with), he couldn't pay me anything close to what I was making at Bunker Hill without "upsetting the scale." No big deal, I said. Like Prince Harry starting with a lowly commission in the RAF, I was already a kind of princeling. This was merely the first tiny sword I had to fall on.

PRIVILEGE HAS A COST.

CHAPTER 23
ASSISTANT TO THE PRESIDENT

With the exception of the rare coin or bullion purchase at IPMC, I had spent my entire business career in high-rise buildings selling things I never touched. Even the railcars of metal I sold at Bunker Hill became numeric entries on a sales log. Working at a South Side of Chicago manufacturing firm that actually made things was unlike anything I had ever done before, and settling in wasn't as simple as I had anticipated.

The company headquarters near Midway Airport consisted of a one-story office building, a sprawling warehouse, and a factory full of plastic injection molding machines. There were offices for executives, sales, and factory management, some with computers, surrounded by an open area with desks for secretaries and order takers. The company manufactured a line of hooks and plastic bathroom fixtures that were packaged and sent all over the world. The name, Selfix, implied these were products you could put up yourself, as in "self-fix."

ANY DOUBLE ENTENDRE WITH "THERAPY" WAS ENTIRELY UNINTENTIONAL.

Most of the employees in the office were Irish Catholics, while the factory was a mix of African-American and Hispanic workers, with a small contingent of Polish immigrants. Mike's brother-in-law, Maurie, was head of sales and my mother-in-law, Norma, was Vice President of Anything She Wanted to Be. There were a couple young Jewish guys too. Andy in purchasing dressed like John Travolta in *Saturday Night Fever*, with the open shirt and the gold chain resting on a thatch of chest hair, and Tom in sales wore thick glasses and a wig for reasons no one ever explained.

One foreshadowing indication about how hard the job would be came when "Uncle" Maurie made a crack that I might make a good Selfix executive in ten years. What the hell was he talking about? I wondered. Did he mean if I *survived* for ten years?

Shortly after I started, Mike took me on a sales trip to England, just the two of us. **Traveling with Mike was an odd mix of luxury and penny-pinching.** We flew over on a supersonic Concorde flight, getting to Heathrow in a mere 3.5 hours.

He booked us lodging at the five-star Ritz-Carlton, but in a shared room, a first for me on a business trip.

Several omens of trouble occurred during this trip, but perhaps the one that stood out the most was when we were crossing the street on a busy afternoon. London streets are as crowded as New York's, so it's easy to fall into a one-behind-the-other way of walking. At one point, Mike turned around abruptly, his face twisted in panic looking for me. It was the face you'd see on someone who lost their five-year-old. In that moment, I realized that by joining the company, I went from being the guy who "should be president" to an over-educated nincompoop. Was this what Tom Hagen, the non-Italian son-in-law had to go through when he joined Vito Corleone's gang? **I began to wonder who I'd have to kill to prove myself.**

When I got home from London, I trudged up to our third-floor loft and, in a moment that became significant for Judith and me over the years, I hugged her. "I feel so sorry for you," I said. She replied that she felt I understood, possibly for the first time, some of the ambivalent feelings she had for her family, which was an unexpected and long-term benefit of working for her dad.

> IT MIGHT HAVE EVEN MADE THE WHOLE EXCRUCIATING FOUR YEARS WORTH IT.

CHAPTER 24
PRODUCT DEVELOPMENT

Big surprise. Things got worse before they got better. For starters, Mike and I had a business culture clash. The way I had done things (successfully) in my previous jobs seemed to piss him off. He would burst into my office, not caring who was hearing and spitting with anger. "Goddammit," he'd yell, "this isn't IBM!" Any rebuke Mike made to anyone was always done in the public arena. Shaming was part of the culture.

It took me awhile to figure out that, according to Mike, much of my experience in "big business" was irrelevant in a scrappy, bare knuckles, family-owned manufacturing firm. Plus, Mike believed Jews were smarter than Gentiles—end of story. "Don't think like a *goy*!" he'd snap when I would suggest any kind of win-win strategy. Eventually, Mike and I came to a truce, which meant I moved away from whatever "assistant to the president" was supposed to mean and was put in charge of Product Development, a risky move on his part.

Thankfully, there were parts of the job that I excelled at. In fact, working in product development was probably one of the best jobs I ever had in terms of aligning my skills and interests. It required me to study markets, think about how people lived (channeling my lifelong fascination with anthropology), and use all my people skills to move our projects along.

Selfix had an elaborate costing system for new products, but it was clunky and time consuming. Their bill of materials (BOMs) were just handwritten sheets, which someone had to walk around to various uncooperative employees trying to get them to define how many of this or that imaginary product they could assemble in an hour. Then you had to get similar commitments from the purchasing department for costs of materials, after which you had to chase down the sales guys for estimates on how many they thought we could sell. Bottom line: it was a people game. To get good numbers, you had to work your contacts, cajoling them to give decent answers in a timely manner.

The real problem with this budget model was that anyone could kill your project by shooting out a labor cost that sounded too high, or a sales estimate that was too low. Once you had your cost sheets, you had to prioritize the projects and present them in a meeting where you had to fight for your favorites. This required presentation skills, a little persuasive finesse, charm, and a touch of arrogance.

LUCKILY, I WAS PRETTY GOOD AT IT.

Our computers at this time were still mostly mainframes—big, clunky, inaccessible beasts, guarded by a manager with backlogs of reports to run. When our offices started to buy advanced word processors, they had primitive computing programs built into them, which meant the cost sheets went through endless iterations every time anyone changed one variable.

Frustrated, I used my skills to program the word processor to do the calculations, and when I casually unveiled these crisp printed reports—a huge improvement over the handwritten sheets—it was one of the few times I ever saw Mike at a loss for words. **"Where did these come from?" he sputtered, as if his nincompoop son-in-law sent the top-secret cost sheets to an outside vendor to make these nice reports.** He was dumbfounded when I calmly explained I was using our own in-house capabilities that no one even knew we had.

One of my most shining accomplishments as head of Product Development was managing to get some of my favorite "secretaries" promoted to administrative assistant jobs . . .

EARNING THEIR TRUST AND LOYALTY FOR MY ENTIRE STAY AT THE COMPANY.

CHAPTER 25
MAN OF THE WORLD

For a small company, Selfix was unusually active internationally. Mike and Norma believed in a "hands-on" approach to both buying and selling, and regularly went all over the world to do both, entertaining buyers in Europe, Asia, the Middle East, and South Africa. On top of selling products they manufactured, they beefed up their product lines with items they designed and had manufactured in Hong Kong and Taiwan. Part of my education was to accompany them on these journeys, eventually traveling on my own.

On one expedition, they took both Judith and me to Hong Kong, Taiwan, Singapore, and Australia. Until Judith and I went to Fiji at the end, I didn't do much touristy stuff. I mostly sat in back rooms, drinking tea or alcohol, discussing things related to our business. I also worked trade shows in Birmingham, UK, and Munich, where part of my job was shooing "Asians" off our booth, as my bosses assumed they were only there to "steal ideas." I tried to caution them that it was possible they could be legitimate buyers from Target, but they waved my rookie objection away.

One time in Taipei, Judith, her parents, and I took a stroll after dinner to the Street of Snakes, where they flay live snakes and drain their blood into cups for immediate medicinal consumption. We were the only Caucasians in the crowd around the main performer, who took a long brown snake out of a cage, cut off its head, drained the blood, and pointed to me. "This is for you, blue eyes!" he said. **I declined but later wondered if I should have drunk the magic potion.**

Mike and Norma created blueprints and specifications for the products, then sent them to the overseas vendors to get quotes and order prototypes during their combination selling and buying trips. But as we grew larger, they reluctantly delegated the job to John—our in-house industrial designer—and me.

We bought vinyl-coated wire goods (mostly shower caddies) from Taiwan, where Mike earned the name Shower Caddy King. We also designed refrigerator magnets with Hong Kong vendors. Most of our vendors were small trading companies that contracted out to even smaller factories to make our products, then they would be shipped to us on containers that could be transferred from ship to rail.

On one trip to Taiwan, I toured factories that would qualify as sweatshops, with sparks flying from welding machines run by moms as kids played nearby on the dirt floor.

THOUGH THAT SIGHT WAS UNSETTLING, IT WAS NEVERTHELESS A HEADY FEELING BEING A "MAN OF THE WORLD" ON MY OWN IN ASIA.

Along with the routine work that needed to be accomplished overseas, we often had some kind of problem with a vendor that had to be negotiated. A shipment of refrigerator magnets might arrive with the metal discs popped out, and our internal quality control guy would reject the shipment for safety concerns. Sometimes, Mike would wake me up at 4 AM and start yelling at me on a speakerphone with his "henchmen" gathered about, all eager to earn points by piling on. I had often been drinking and attending lavish dinners and nightclubs with vendors the night before, so I was not in the best shape to deal with an ambush. **I still have nightmares about these wake-up attacks.**

But "fight or flight" was the management style, so I began to practice yelling on my drive to the South Side from my hip downtown loft. That's when I began to wonder if it was good for my health to remain on the job. In fact, not too long afterward, I decided I couldn't take it anymore. I didn't see a future where I could relax into an upper management role and lead a kind of normal executive lifestyle. I now understood why Mike's sons couldn't hack it there. I had held on as long as possible, but in the end, the daily ordeal was just too much for me. It was also hard on Judith. But how to tell Mike and Norma I was leaving?

We decided to have them over to our loft for a homemade dinner, where I told Mike bluntly that if I didn't leave, I would end up hating him. These were difficult, but well-chosen words. He instantly understood it was over and switched gears to how we'd make the transition to my departure. **He shocked—and relieved—me by asking what was best for me.**

Some years later, I had a very satisfying phone call with Mike, when he told me he had found some write-ups I had done about the industry while reconnoitering a housewares show. It included predictions and recommendations for where we could go as a company, and what product lines might be good to expand into. **Mike said all my predictions had come true.**

I CHOKED UP; IT WAS A RARE EMOTIONAL MOMENT BETWEEN US.

CHAPTER 26
DICKENS DESIGN

I had been worried about financial insecurity since the hippie days (and before), but now I had this new hybrid resume—half metals, half product development in an entirely different industry. Plus, I wanted my transition from Selfix to happen fast and was focused on a "story" that made sense for my leaving. It was uncomfortable being a "lame duck," where everyone knew I was moving on because I couldn't hack their tough boss.

I was accustomed to being an executive—with an executive salary. I had no interest in returning to the metals business, and four years in various capacities in a housewares company didn't show me a clear path. But I got an idea.

Selfix would occasionally hire creative firms to supplement their design process. This primarily happened before we had our own department, but I had met some of these guys. Their designs were usually presented by the boss/owner, who was a slick Michigan Avenue type. I had even been to one of their offices, Joss Design. It felt like an upscale ad agency, a cool place to work. But where would I fit in a firm like this? I wasn't a real product designer with a degree in engineering. The only thing that linked my resumes together was selling—or to use the fancier word, "marketing."

I wondered if perhaps I could parlay my meager knowledge of design and housewares into a job with one of these industrial design firms. I reached out and some of the firms seemed interested. I suspected they might see me as a conduit to business they might get from Selfix, as they knew I was Mike's son-in-law. I didn't want to imply that I could promise that, so I had to walk a line. I finally landed an interview with an interesting firm, Dickens Design.

Their office comprised an entire freestanding Frank Lloyd Wright-style building just off Michigan Avenue, within walking distance of our downtown loft. The building had probably been a cutting-edge showpiece once. It was quirky and intriguing, but it was easy to see where maintenance or renovation might help.

My meeting was with the venerable Mr. Dickens, a white-haired patriarch who had a grand, self-important manner tempered with a touch of wry humor. He reminded me of some of the "self-made men" in the battery business. He grandly explained they had been the first packaging firm to use black on a food package: Minute Maid Orange Juice Concentrate.

I liked the idea of selling package design, which relied more on aesthetics than hard-core engineering. Dickens was selling a brand to big consumer companies, not unlike the ones I had called on in the metals business. I felt I could handle the patriarch after putting up with Mike. Then came the hitch.

"I'll be leaving for Florida soon," Mr. Dickens said. "My son, Bob, will be in charge." Translation: he was hiring someone to "help out" his kid. **The subtle implication of incompetence was a red flag I conveniently missed.**

Bob was much older than I expected, maybe early fifties. A short, plump man with a creepy giggle, he was full of nervous tics, the kind of guy you veer away from at a cocktail party. His hobbies included fussing over a couple of spoiled dachshunds and trying to build expensive Lotus automobiles from "kits." My job was to fill in the gaps where Bob fell short.

While Dickens (Senior) agreed to my salary request, he asked casually if it would be acceptable if I worked "only on new business." This was a second red flag I didn't see. I figured Dickens Design was an established firm with a good (if dated) portfolio and an impressive (if past its prime) building. How hard would it be to get new business?

IT WASN'T LONG BEFORE I REALIZED I HAD MADE ANOTHER CAREER BLUNDER.

First, I determined that Bob Dickens was clinically insane. When a client needed to get to O'Hare from our office, Bob suggested he drive him in "one of his Lotuses." I think Bob saw himself as a sort of James Bond/MacGyver man-of-the-world who could pilot a helicopter without a lesson. Bob neglected to tell the client that the Lotus didn't have a steering wheel. According to Bob's retelling, he had no problem steering the vehicle with a vise grip wrench in Chicago's rush hour traffic. When the client decided to cease doing business with us, Bob was puzzled and looked to blame his staff of artists.

At that point, I couldn't imagine staying with Dickens. After Judith and I talked through what we really wanted to do, I made my decision to leave and . . .

SHE MADE HER CASE FOR MOVING BACK TO MINNEAPOLIS BECAUSE... WHY THE HELL NOT?

CHAPTER 27
ILLUSTRATOR

We had one friend in Chicago who was making a full-time living as an illustrator. His name was David Csiscko, and he had graduated from the Art Institute. His distinctive silhouette style—slightly punk with a touch of Art Deco—was affording him steady work and landing his art in places like *Chicago Magazine*.

Knowing about my *Reader* cartoons, David brought up the idea of me going freelance as an illustrator. I might not have taken it as seriously if David hadn't generously set me up with one of his own clients.

"JUST TAKE SOME DRAWINGS OVER THERE AND SEE WHAT THEY SAY," HE SAID.

His client was a friendly young woman who edited several publications for the American Bar Association, located nearby on Michigan Avenue. One of their publications was *Student Lawyer*, obviously geared toward a hip young audience. I was stunned when she immediately commissioned a few drawings. It was a bit shocking to think that after all these years of trying to be a businessman by day and artist by night, I had stumbled onto a profession that combined creativity, humor, and an ability to talk to people.

Other than the cartoons for *The Chicago Reader*, I had never sold my creative output before—and I really didn't know what I was doing. I also wasn't confident that my drawing skills had a range beyond what I liked to draw.

A plan took shape to market my quirky pen-and-ink drawings as a "signature style," hoping to bypass any need to draw clip-art. I didn't realize that most illustrators start out drawing chickens (i.e., anything the client wants) and work toward a signature style they push to become their trademark as they get more successful. Years later, I was told: "You never wanted to just draw a chicken." So as we prepared the move back to Minneapolis, I started to reimagine myself as a self-employed illustrator.

WAS IT THE DREAM CAREER I WAS ALWAYS MEANT TO HAVE?

CHAPTER 28
COMPUTER ART

When the first Apple computer went on the market, I jumped on it. I delighted in its graphics programs, however crude they seem now by today's standards. The idea of partnering with a machine to create a drawing was intriguing, and it was a way of utilizing chance in that it was difficult to control.

On a whim, I sent a drawing of dinosaurs and a volcano to a contest at *Macworld Magazine*, a big deal publication at the time. I won first prize, which turned out to be a gigantic printer that was more sophisticated than anything I had encountered. Its market value was around $5,000 (which is closer to $13,000 today), so I ended up selling it, but not before counting on it as a "sign from the gods" that the illustration path was a Good Idea.

Once we settled back in Minneapolis, I tried to get unemployment from Dickens. But unless one had a grievance for voluntary departure, you couldn't get it if you quit. I tried to make the case that they had made it "difficult for me to succeed" there, which was actually true. I even had a lawyer friend on the call, but to no avail. In the end, I felt slightly guilty that I had left on good terms, then tried to wriggle some compensation out of it.

Doing illustration as a real job turned out to be intimidating. Judith encouraged me to go to art school to learn the trade, and it was probably good advice, but it seemed to push the problem of making money so far into a mythical future that it was hard to see how it would help my current anxiety. My plan was to deal with my panic by "getting serious" about selling myself as an illustrator. Like many times before, I asked, "How hard can it be?"

HUBRIS TO THE RESCUE.

I did take a few computer and video production classes at the Minneapolis College of Art and Design (MCAD) before Photoshop took over the world. MCAD had a bunch of prototype graphic computers donated by manufacturers (many of which have since gone out of business), and the teacher walked the class through the basics of each machine. Unfortunately, her cursory lessons resulted in most of the output being far from impressive. I did, however, make friends with the computer staff, and when I heard they were looking for someone to teach the Extension Class, I volunteered. They surprised me by saying yes.

Suddenly, I was a teacher at the prestigious Minneapolis College of Art and Design—and without an art degree!

I also became friends with a graphic design teacher named Colette who was bitten by the computer bug too. We discovered there was an art supply manufacturer in the western US named Artograph that had an underutilized but "advanced" graphic computer. Artograph devices to project images for tracing were well established in the art market. Colette and I met with the president and he invited us to see his Wasatch computer, named for mountains in Idaho. The Wasatch was one step above the clunky prototypes in the MCAD lab, but they didn't know how to promote it. The idea of letting us use the software to debug and develop commercial applications for it was appealing to all parties. So the president let us use it "for free" until we were making money, at which time we'd presumably renegotiate our deal. Colette designed us a logo, and I named our company Technographica.

Sadly, there were myriad problems with this level of graphic computer. Not only was there little subtlety to the images, as everything was constructed with clunky polygons, but the output was problematic: slides rendered individually and slowly. Yet another issue was convincing commercial clients (ad agencies or in-house marketing departments) how to use the slides in their production of end products. People weren't selling computer graphics yet, and art departments wanted traditional art, airbrushed drawings, marker sketches, and paintings.

I continued to teach at MCAD, though my knowledge of computer graphics was minimal. Mostly, I hoped no one showed up who knew more than I did. **Eventually, someone did.**

Mark Jones owned a state-of-the-art computer lab in his suburban home that was much better than anything the school had, even more sophisticated than the Wasatch.

Artograph management was getting impatient with us, as we were treading water with no tangible results. Independently wealthy via inheritance, Mark had great equipment, though it was unclear what he intended to do with it. He had done an apprenticeship with a prestigious *National Geographic* photographer—the one who did the famous young Afghan girl for the cover—but as yet hadn't found his perfect niche.

Mark invited me to use his house and equipment—a PC-based graphics board called Targa, which sold for about $5,000. Despite being an "Apple guy" (for what it was worth at the time) and knowing nothing about the DOS-based PCs, I bought my own Targa system.

IT WAS A BIG COMMITMENT, BUT ONE THAT PAID OFF.

I soon learned that Targa's forte was compositing scanned photographs. This appealed to me for two reasons. First, the results looked awesome and were difficult to do outside of a darkroom at the time. Second, it got me away from my problem of not being able (or willing) to "draw a chicken." Instead, I could make montages, with little drawing involved.

I began to sell illustrations and Mark managed to get jobs as well. Sometimes, the easiest ones came with big price tags. One company paid us $5,000 to take an image of the Earth and do simple manipulations, like you can do on your phone today. I was commissioned to do a cover for the *Utne Reader*, a national magazine. And a local printing company, Bolger Press, hired me to make promotional posters for them. **They treated me with a great respect, like I was a cutting-edge artist.**

IT LOOKED LIKE A WORLD I COULD POSSIBLY LIVE IN.

CHAPTER 29
PRODUCT DEVELOPMENT CONSULTANT

It's hard to put my finger on why illustration didn't become my "final career." Creating art for money, as it turned out, was more difficult than I imagined for several reasons. Finding clients was difficult; satisfying them was also difficult. Getting enough business—and repeat business—was difficult. Doing the montages was difficult. Waiting to get paid was difficult. **Freelance work, in general, was just plain difficult.**

When Photoshop came out a few years later, what we were doing became readily available and cheaper to create on the Mac. I could have adjusted to that, but I was disillusioned with the "perfect job for me." An illustrator was essentially a guy some hotshot young art director told what to draw—and as I said before, I didn't like being told what to draw. I had gone from being an executive who schmoozed with CEOs, traveled internationally, and made deals worth thousands of dollars to being a guy who bristled at being pigeonholed as an artist. But an illustrator was a craftsman and drawing was the bread and butter of its life. My photo collaging was "working," in some sense, but the experiences I had in corporations (even Selfix) seemed to use more of my brain than "making pictures" did. I realized I wasn't as enamored with craftsmanship as I thought.

It was somewhat serendipitous that a new opportunity arose that seemed easier, more lucrative, and oddly more satisfying than illustration: product development consulting. It didn't strike me right away that I had the qualifications for it, but I knew an engineer who worked in the field. Through some circumstances that elude memory, I met his client, Jim, who worked at 3M. When Jim found out I had a background in housewares and was an artist, he thought I might prove useful on one of their projects.

At the time, 3M was studying ways it could use Post-It Note technology in other areas in the home, like decorating walls and windows. Despite knowing little about what a consultant did, I went through 3M's vetting process.

SURPRISINGLY, THEY KNEW OF SELFIX AND WERE CONCERNED ABOUT MY IN-LAW RELATIONSHIP WITH THE OWNERS.

Though they didn't exactly spell it out, they were planning to take over the market for peel-and-stick hooks. I had to convince them that I was no longer associated with Selfix and could keep secrets. Besides, I wasn't to work directly with the hook people, but with the Post-It stationery department.

The amount of money involved dropped my jaw. Even working part-time with renewable contracts, I began to pull in about $70,000 a year. I enjoyed driving to the big corporate headquarters in St. Paul, once again donning a suit, and I felt this was a job I could do for the rest of my life if I played my cards right. Working with a team leader named Arthur, we brainstormed, hired artists, made prototypes, ran focus groups, and wrote up reports. I was transported back to a world where I felt more valued and where people listened to what I had to say. My brain got paid more than my hands—a lesson I first learned back at IPMC.

But then a controversy arose when our project went "over budget." It was news to me that we even had a budget, and if we did, I assumed it was Arthur's job to oversee it. Since I hadn't been properly mentored in how to do this, the controversy hit me by surprise. My "consultant buddies" (including Jim, who originally hired me and had left to work freelance) told me "these things happen," and their advice was to keep my head down for a while until the bosses forgot about the incident. "Give it a little time," they said, "and by the time you come back, there will be different people and no record of a 'problem' with your judgment."

While my blunder did seem to dissipate, I can't deny I felt a bit as if I was being watched for my next misstep. I did learn a lot at 3M about focus groups and the early stages of brainstorming a product, and I could have been quite good at it, but I would have had to learn some things that weren't initially obvious.

Around this time, Judith's parents died and left her (and her siblings) a sizable amount of real estate and investments. With our financial advisor's help, we determined that if we kept our spending "in line," it was possible to live off the interest generated.

This presented a new issue: What was it I really wanted to do? The controversy at 3M left a bad taste, and I didn't love product development consulting enough to keep slaying those particular dragons.

I HOPED SOMEONE WOULD MIRACULOUSLY SHOW UP AND HELP ME FIGURE IT OUT.

CHAPTER 30
BUSINESS TESTING

Mark, the guy who had the photo compositing lab in his suburban home, told me he found a guru who had changed his life. His name was Bob and his company was Business Testing. Bob had given Mark a new life direction after an exhaustive batch of personality tests, and at the "old age" of 35, Mark decided to go to school to become a doctor.

I wondered, could Mark's guru help me? Had my career path been difficult because I had never gotten a proper education? I was skeptical that a company named Business Testing, located in a downtown highrise, could tell me what to do. I could picture Bob, presumably a stern old man, looking over his bifocals and telling me, "Go, get your MBA. It's not too late!" Perhaps an MBA *would* help me become the respectable business person I had been trying to be. **Thinking I had nothing to lose, I went to see what Business Testing would guide me to do.**

Bob sat across from me with his balding head, bushy eyebrows, a piercing stare, and a playful smile. He looked like the photo of Carl Jung on the back cover of *Modern Man in Search of a Soul*. The first thing he said was, "There's something about me you should know." I nodded encouragingly. "I have been diagnosed with terminal cancer." Without missing a beat, he added, "Do you still want to work with me?"

"OF COURSE," I SAID. WHAT KIND OF PERSON WOULD LET THAT GET IN THE WAY? NOT ME.

We started with the tests Mark had talked about. Some people hate tests, but I've always liked them, especially the kind that probe your personality, where there isn't a right answer. Maybe they would reveal something about myself I didn't know.

Ironically, the first one was the Minnesota Multi-Phasic Personality Inventory I had last done at the Residential College at the University of Michigan, the one I made fun of in my movie *The Carrot Test*. When Bob and I met to review my results, I expected solemn news about how I needed more business skills. Instead, Bob looked up from his papers and asked, "What did you want to do in college?"

Without hesitation, I said, "I wanted to be a filmmaker."

"Then you should go to film school!" he announced triumphantly.

WTF? Had I stumbled onto another *Do What You Love and the Money Will Follow* idiot? Hadn't that Follow Your Bliss stuff ruined my generation, teeming as we were with underpaid artists, massage therapists, and past-life regressors? Was Bob's proximity to mortality clouding his once clear-eyed view of the world?

"Film school?" I said. "Like Stephen Spielberg's spoiled grandchildren? I'm a married man. I have a kid. I'm forty-one, for chrissake."

The tests, he said, told him I needed to work with "words and pictures."

Like illustration? Cartooning? Been there, done that.

But Bob was persistent. "Why don't you look into film again?"

AND SO, THAT BECAME MY HOMEWORK.

CHAPTER 31
NOVELIST

A bit relieved that Bob from Business Testing didn't try to talk me into getting an MBA, I began talking to anyone I knew who had anything to do with the film business. Several people suggested that, unless I wanted to be a camera person, an inroad could be to work on my writing.

I took a class in short story crafting at The Loft, a large writing education establishment in Minneapolis. I was lucky to find a teacher, Linda, who encouraged me. She said my first story, *Greenman*—about a corporate guy exploring the Men's Movement—had "something in it to offend everyone." Though offending was not my goal, she also said she read it to her lover in bed and they laughed. My interest in culture clash encouraged me to expand it into a novel, though it somehow veered into alien abduction. When I showed a draft of it to my next teacher, Ian, his face scrunched up. "Yeah, but do you really want to be writing about aliens?" The answer was yes, but I lacked the *chutzpah* to stand up for wackiness in that literary crowd. So I took the characters and reworked them into a plot involving the controversy around a deer kill in a Minnesota park. Without taking sides, my focus was on how each family member looked at it from a very different perspective.

THIS BECAME MY FIRST NOVEL, *CUTE EATS CUTE*.

I managed to get some decent blurbs, one from Joel Hodgson of *Mystery Science Theater 3000*, another from Tim Johnston, a novelist, and a third from Jan Dizard, the author of *Going Wild: Hunting, Animal Rights, and the Contested Meaning of Nature*. I found a local publisher, North Star Press, and though it didn't fit that well with their lineup of books on great churches of Minnesota, I was in print! I later republished it under my own logo of Zoographico Press.

I continued writing, though with a few false starts. One book I wrote was about working for my father-in-law entitled *Shower Caddy King*, and another was about alien abduction called *Land Somewhere Else*. Finally, I completed and self-published my second novel, *The End of Men*, about a group of young filmmakers who reconnect later as adults on a Greek island where things get weird and culty. Unfortunately, the title was used later for a sociological book on feminism and, as I see now, several other novels about men being wiped out by viruses. So much for catchy titles.

A bit discouraged by the difficulty of breaking into the world of literary novels, I decided finally to write something solely for me, something fun. I got the idea of having aliens (yes, they're back!) abduct people and put them inside the actors of notoriously bad science fiction movies, like *Queen of Outer Space* and *Cat-Women of the Moon*. It also incorporated the Heaven's Gate suicide cult but, in my version, they achieved their goal of arriving on a spaceship after death. They didn't encounter the friendly Space Brothers, however, but a rather dictatorial state run by a leader who loved bad old-Earth movies.

When my older son, Nicolas, read it, he said, "Your main character doesn't want anything." My other son, Lucas, agreed it lacked tension. Since Nicolas had specific ideas about it, we basically co-authored a rewrite. It ended up being four books: *Tarzan in the Bardo, Northwoods Bardo, Bardoworld* . . .

> AND THE FOURTH, BARDO ZSA ZSA, I LEFT STANDING OUTSIDE THE TRILOGY ON ITS OWN.

CHAPTER 32
PAINTER

My graphic art, up to this point, consisted primarily of cartooning and the drawings for my Zoographico artist books. During the time I lived in Chicago, our social group was comprised mainly of performance artists, dancers, and a few painters. Despite living in Chicago during the ascendancy of Hairy Who (Roger Brown, Jim Nutt, etc.), I didn't have much of an impulse to paint. The Hairy Who group's embrace of pop culture was portrayed in comics, posters, and ads with an ironic sense of humor, reflecting a punk version of Warhol's enchantment with commercial art (like soup cans). Though my sensibility was a good fit, the few times I tried to paint, I wasn't able to conjure the relaxed improvisation I felt when drawing, and I would often end up painting over what I had done. When I got critiques from artist friends, their classic "art school" concerns of composition and color left me uninspired.

Fast-forward five years to Minneapolis. I was now the father of two small boys. Judith and I bought two plain wooden stools so they could stand at the sink and brush their teeth, and I thought it would be fun if the stools were decorated with playful animal motifs. I considered hiring an artist friend to do it—but I hesitated. Why couldn't I just paint the stools? I had been schlepping my acrylics around for years but had felt no impulse to paint. Surprisingly, my paints hadn't completely dried up, so I turned the stools into naïve scenes with jungle animals, volcanos, and intertwining tree roots.

IT WAS SHOCKINGLY FUN.

I began painting small canvases, borrowing content from my "studies" of the Knights Templar, the occult, Aleister Crowley, and alchemy. I deliberately mixed all the elements with mischievous playfulness into pseudo-meaningful compositions, an ironic approach to content I still use. Somewhat later, I discovered this was called pop surrealism, roughly defined as narrative elements in non-narrative arrangements. It was similar to the way surrealism and Dada worked, mining the unconscious.

Pop surrealism has an affinity with "outsider art," a category that grew out of Jean Dubuffet's post-WWII interest in grouping the art of children with the art of the insane. The category includes religious visionaries like Howard Finster, and others like Adolfi Wolfi and Henry Darger, who were considered marginally sane at best. I have always found outsider or visionary work more inspiring in many ways than contemporary art. The popularity of the genre has expanded its ranks to include artists who admire and emulate the visionary style, whether or not they attended art school, such as self-taught Joe Coleman, who paints like R. Crumb on darker drugs (and who keeps trying to get into the New York Outsider Art Fair by claiming he was kicked out of art school).

When we moved to Marine on St. Croix, our house had two garages. One was attached, and the previous owner had used it for country boy toys, like ATVs and motorcycles. We took the stand-alone garage for cars and I inherited the heated garage for a studio. At first it seemed enormous, even intimidating. I'd never had a "real studio" before, and eventually I took it over by adding furniture, a wood-burning stove, a TV, and lots and lots of tchotchkes.

I bumbled around a bit with content and themes until I hit on the idea of painting in a series. I wanted a strong enough idea that could endure through several paintings so I didn't have to be constantly thinking about what would come next. I meandered through various subject matter: science fiction, magic, mythical creatures, occult charts. One series was based on playing cards, another was portraits of world leaders, and a third was inspired by vintage stage-magic posters.

While I have managed to get into numerous shows all over the country, the concept of "selling" remains elusive.

> **FOR THE VISIONARY LONER WORKING IN HIS GARAGE, IT'S AKIN TO TALKING TO ALIENS.**

CHAPTER 33
PRISON ART TEACHER

Despite penitentiaries looming large in the mythical landscape of movies and TV, I didn't set out to be a prison art teacher. Judith was teaching prison meditation classes through her Zen Center, and one of her fellow teachers walked through my art studio one day and said, "You should do something in the prisons."

Something, but what? Not long after, I saw an article in the local paper about the art class at Stillwater Prison and reached out to the new teacher, Jeff Guse. He expressed enthusiasm, but before I was allowed to become a volunteer, I had to take a two-week basic safety class. It was all fascinating—especially learning how to press the panic button on my walkie-talkie that would call a SWAT team.

Stillwater is a level 4 high-security prison. (There is only one level 5 prison in the state, in nearby Oak Park Heights that is reserved for serial killers and inmates prone to violence.) The "art students" ranged from ages twenty to seventy and spanned the ethnic spectrum of African-Americans, Native Americans, Asians (Hmong and Thai), and Africans (Somalis and Sudanese). The Caucasians made up maybe twenty percent, but it was all in constant flux. The whites often had the shaved-head and neck-tatted look of *Sons of Anarchy*, though technically no gang affiliations were allowed in the education program. Their crimes ranged from drug dealing, robbery, and kidnapping, to sexual assault and murder. One generally didn't ask about their crimes, though sometimes they volunteered some of the gory details.

SOMETIMES WHEN YOU HEARD WHAT SOMEONE DID, YOU IMMEDIATELY WISHED YOU HADN'T.

As I was introducing myself on my first day, a young Cuban American "leader type," straightforwardly asked, "Why are you here?" I wasn't prepared for a challenging question, and I fumbled a bit for an answer. I don't remember exactly what I said, but thankfully I avoided saying anything about "wanting to help." **I learned later that "helping" was anathema. They hate feeling patronized or pitied.**

The art room was brightly lit and modern, with twenty-five art stations consisting of tables and easels. There were two lockable rooms—one for supplies the "tutors" (inmates elevated to positions of responsibility) had access to, and my colleague Jeff's office. Jeff was a pleasant man with a dry sense of humor. His atypical resume included working at a nuclear plant and being a trained prison guard, on top of earning a fine arts degree.

Education was categorized as a job for the inmates, though with an extremely low hourly "wage." It was also considered a privilege. Any infraction—rule-breaking, fighting, "hooch" brewing, tattoo paraphernalia—would remove you from the class, and it could take months to work your way back in. Despite many other jobs paying more, the casual ambiance of the room was desirable to many inmates. Jeff even streamed music, and unless it got out of hand, the guys were free to wander around and talk.

The expectation of our students was to sit at their desks and "make art" for the entire day. Jeff gave individualized instruction for the new guys in the basics of art theory. While Jeff had a wide appreciation of art, the program by necessity focused on teachable skills. This tended to support the "old fashioned" idea that a painting was either a still life, landscape, or portrait.

The inmates knew I was a practicing artist, and I would show some of them my self-published books. Generally, their education was so inadequate they had no sense of what role art played in the real world. For example, a guy once tried to describe what he called a gallery: "You know, the one with the big lions out front." I assumed this meant the Minneapolis Art Institute and tactfully tried to explain the difference between a museum and a gallery.

"Are you in there?" he asked.

"Not yet," I replied.

Despite their lack of knowledge, however, on more than one occasion, guys would come in who could copy a photograph using a graphite pencil and get near photo-realistic results. One of my self-assigned roles was to "defend" non-representational art. Some of the inmates' experiences supported the non-representational, as their contact with graphics might come through graffiti or tattooing. I encouraged anyone who showed any desire to find their personal style, and I came up with my own way of teaching, including principles like "Don't be afraid to wreck a piece," and "Good art is something you can look at for a long time."

In the early years of my teaching, our department had to conduct a "Building Character" class once a week. Jeff asked me if we could do it on Tuesday afternoons when I came in. I agreed but struggled to gather a quorum of five to six guys from the larger group.

SOMETIMES IT WORKED BETTER THAN OTHER TIMES.

If we had an "alpha" who liked to talk, he would encourage others to come to the table. The class consisted of a handout to read and a topic like compassion to discuss. While the authors tried to make it relevant to prison life, the guys often joked they were written by "Christians in Oklahoma."

Originally, I expected to follow the once-a-month model my wife's meditation group used. But after my first day, Jeff asked me if I wanted to come back the next week. I said yes, and I've been going there one afternoon a week for eleven years . . .

UNTIL THE COVID PANDEMIC IN 2020.

EPILOGUE

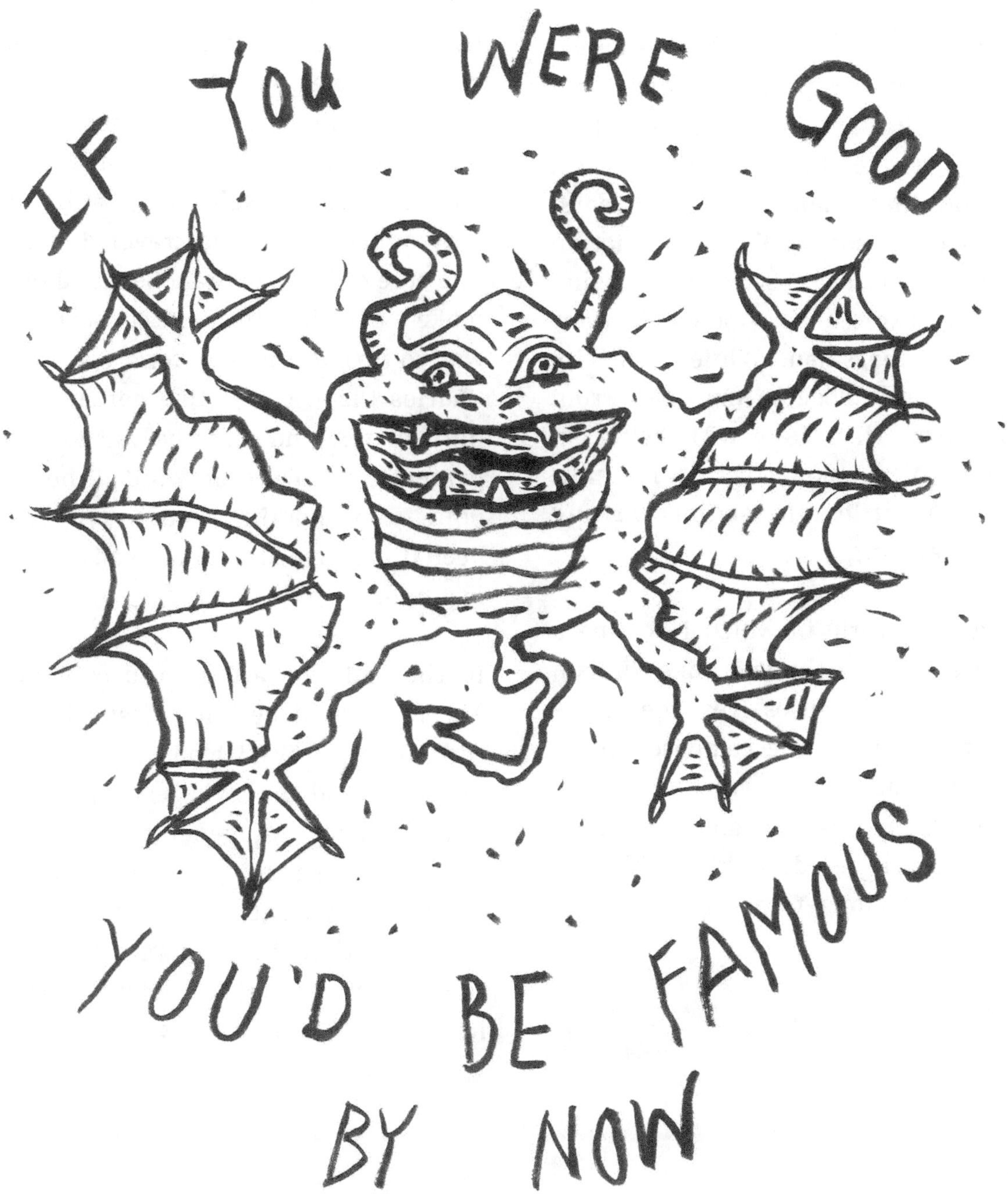
IF YOU WERE GOOD
YOU'D BE FAMOUS
BY NOW

I know one thing for sure: not everything turns out like you expect. As much as I scorned my father's "simplistic" idea that one just "picks a good career" (in his case, dentist), now that I am in my late years, I see its practical wisdom. Partly in reaction to his premise, I never seriously considered the "big careers" of Doctor, Lawyer, or Serious Businessman. While creativity and the arts were close to my heart from childhood, after flirtations with being an "underground filmmaker," it took me until my forties to settle into serious writing and playful painting.

I can imagine a world in which I became a doctor and a poet on the side, like William Carlos Williams, or Charles Ives, the insurance executive avant-garde composer, but I have no regrets about the path I've chosen. As I was discussing this book and my eclectic job life over seven decades with Judith, she asked, "In lieu of a long-term career, what do you have?"

"EXPERIENCES," I SAID WITHOUT HESITATION.

Had I been that single-focused doctor (the closest fantasy to "the career that got away"), I might not have been a hippie, underground filmmaker, nude model, janitor, metals salesman, and product development guy who traveled the world. The tree of life has branches, and once you make a decision, the next concern is which way to turn at the next fork. Or as the poet Charles Olson said, "One perception must immediately and directly lead to a further perception." In other words, there is no point in wondering who you might have been if you turned right instead of left at the last node.

In the end, you are a child of your time. My father's generation (especially after the horror of WWII) had stability, steady progress, and the civic respect due a solid "family man." My generation was asking, "Who do you really want to be? And what do you really want to do?" Of course, being young, we thought these were "better questions" than what the previous generations had asked. **What I see now is that each generation asks new questions.**

As Gertrude Stein said, "Nothing changes in people from one generation to another except the way of seeing and being seen." I suppose it's no surprise, then, that I've come to witness my kids' generation having issues with the questions (and answers) my Boomer generation engaged. In the words of Kurt Vonnegut...

"SO IT GOES."

ABOUT THE AUTHOR

Obviously, C.B. Murphy has had a lot of jobs. These days he spends most of his time writing fiction and painting. He has written several novels, including *Cute Eats Cute*, and is currently working on *The Bardo Trilogy*, a series of science fiction novels. You can view his art on www.cbmurphy.net and Instagram (@cb_murphy).

www.ingramcontent.com/pod-product-compliance
Lightning Source LLC
Chambersburg PA
CBHW080347300426
44110CB00019B/2528